The Films of
TOMMY LEE JONES

Samuel Goldwyn Presents

Robert Mitchum on the Screen

The Films of Anthony Quinn (*Citadel*)

The Films of Sidney Poitier (*Citadel*)

The Complete Films of Tyrone Power (*coauthor; Citadel*)

The Complete Films of Edward G. Robinson (*Citadel*)

Katharine Hepburn: A Pictorial Study

Boris Karloff: A Pictorial

Errol Flynn: A Pictorial

Movies Made for Television (1964–*PRESENT*)

More Theatre: Stage to Screen to Television

The Ultimate John Wayne Trivia Book (*Citadel*)

Moe Howard & the 3 Stooges (*editor*) (*Citadel*)

The Films of
TOMMY LEE JONES

ALVIN H. MARILL

A Citadel Press Book

PUBLISHED BY CAROL PUBLISHING GROUP

A Citadel Press Book
Published by Carol Publishing Group

Citadel Press is a registered trademark of Carol
Communications, Inc.

Editorial, sales and distribution, and rights and permissions
    inquiries should be addressed to Carol Publishing Group,
    120 Enterprise Avenue, Secaucus, N.J. 07094
In Canada: Canadian Manda Group, One Atlantic Avenue,
    Suite 105, Toronto, Ontario M6K 3E7

Carol Publishing Group books may be purchased in bulk at
special discounts for sales promotion, fund-raising, or
educational purposes. Special editions can be created to
specifications. For details, contact: Special Sales Department,
Carol Publishing Group, 120 Enterprise Avenue, Secaucus,
N.J. 07094

Designed by A. Christopher Simon

Manufactured in the United States of America

10 9 8 7 6 5 4 3 2 1

LIBRARY OF CONGRESS CATALOGING-IN-PUBLICATION DATA

Marill, Alvin H.
    The films of Tommy Lee Jones / Alvin H. Marill.
        p.   cm.
    "A Citadel Press book."
    ISBN 0-8065-1952-5 (pbk.)
    1. Jones, Tommy Lee, 1946-   . I. Title.
PN2287.J64M37   1996
791.43′028′092—dc20
                                                    95-48051
                                                    CIP

Acknowledgments

The supporting cast, without whom there would be no book on Tommy Lee Jones, includes, alphabetically, John Cocchi, Rob Edelman, Jane Klain, David McGillivray, James Robert Parish, Lee Pfeiffer, Jerry Vermilye (and his terrific photo collection), and my editor, Allan J. Wilson, as well as Sandy, a.k.a. Mrs. M. And a nod to the Museum of Television and Radio, Lincoln Center Library for the Performing Arts, Jerry Ohlinger's Movie Material Store, and Movie Star News in New York; to Film Favorites in Oklahoma; and to the British Film Institute in London.

Contents

The Films of
TOMMY LEE JONES

The Road from San Saba to Harvard to Manhattan and L.A.

Tommy has an unerring sense for the poetry of life that is not apparent to someone who simply sees [his taciturnity].

—Al Gore (in the *Washington Post*)

He is definitely the kind of man who would have ridden with Sam Houston to the Alamo. He is very strong in his beliefs and close to the land.

—Oliver Stone

Actor, polo player, Texas cattle rancher, oil-field rigger, poet, "the Southwest Bogart," as *Time*'s Richard Corliss refers to him. Peter Bogdanovich has described him as "Bronson with a touch of Montgomery Clift." Certainly not a tumbleweed-kicking cowpoke.

Tommy Lee Jones, "whose glare," Tony Scott, *Daily Variety*'s television critic, once wrote, "could stop a charging rhino," has been redefining his craft on stage, screen, and TV for three decades now and has become, like Gene Hackman, an effortless "actor's actor" and, in the process, a shameless scene-stealer. Rough-hewn, craggy-faced, exuding sheer masculinity, a definite sexuality, and a no-nonsense manner, Tommy Lee Jones is not to be confused in any way with Tom Jones the singer and Vegas entertainer or Tom Jones *The Fantasticks*

At leisure during his New York days of the early 1970s

In Manhattan with first wife, Katherine Lardner

composer or Tommy Lee the nineties rock idol, to say nothing of rocker Rickie Lee Jones. "Movie star, hell. You get well known a little bit and that word crops up," the normally media-shy "Texas" Tommy Lee told the *San Francisco Sunday Examiner and Chronicle* in 1981, about ten years into his career. "I don't want to be a movie star, I want to be a successful actor."

Following are the Tommy Lee Jones basics: An eighth-generation Texan, he was born on September 15, 1946, in San Saba (the term "hardscrabble" usually appears here in most articles about Jones), was raised around horses and still lives in that West Texas town, which is about eighty miles northwest of Austin. His dad, hard-drinking Clyde L. Jones, worked in the oil fields, at home and in Libya; his mother, Lucille Marie Scott (known as Marie), was a policewoman who came from a rodeo family. The marriage reportedly was quite abusive, and Clyde and Marie divorced and rewed during their son's early days. When Tommy Lee was three, Marie had another son, who died in infancy. (Much of this flies in the face of the fanciful biographical data put forth by several entertainment journalists about his growing up in a dirt-floored shack, the son of "poor white trash," probably bull Jones, reticent around writers, dished out early in his career.)

"Both my mother and father used to go to honky-tonk bars," Jones related to Lillian Ross for an article in *The New Yorker*, "to do what everybody in that part of Texas did—drink. I'd wait for them outside in the car, alone. I remember hearing music and singing coming through the walls of the saloon to me in the car. I remember lying there, just waiting, just waiting, alone."

Tommy Lee and Katherine Lardner Jones

Tommy Lee grew up working for a while at the Hughes Tool Company (who could know at the time that he'd one day play Howard Hughes and "own" Hughes Tool?) and in the oil fields, with his father and without him. Clyde died of a heart attack in his mid-fifties. Marie remarried and now lives in Cameron, about 110 miles east of San Saba. Tommy Lee himself started playing tackle football at the age of thirteen while at Alamo Junior High in Midland. Later, he went to St. Mark's School of Texas, a Dallas prep school, where he not only continued playing football but also drifted into acting. "One day I happened to walk into a practice room and came upon a rehearsal of *Mister Roberts*. Almost immediately, I started acting in plays—*Under Milk Wood, The Caine Mutiny Court-Martial*. My feelings at this discovery were indescribable."

In 1965, it was off to Harvard, where he played football as offensive guard and won all–Ivy League and all-East honors (he was part of that tie game with archrival Yale that led to the famous *Crimson* headline "Harvard Beats Yale 29–29"), acted in the Harvard Drama Club (which led to his first screen role, as one of Ryan O'Neal's roommates in *Love Story*, which was being filmed at the school), and graduated in 1969 cum laude in English and American literature. Although he was O'Neal's fictional roomie in the movie, he was a real-life roommate of one Albert Gore, who went into politics, and John Lithgow, another actor of note.

Jones and Lithgow did some summer rep in Cambridge and Boston during those years, along with Stockard Channing of Radcliffe and James Woods of MIT. "We did everything, anything. Shakespeare, Brecht, the Greeks." (Interviewers have been cautioned against getting Jones started on James Joyce, Keats, and Aristotle, on whom Tommy Lee is something of an authority.)

Following Harvard, pursuing an acting career in New York, Tom Lee Jones (as he billed himself initially) made his professional stage debut in a bit part—actually six bit parts—in John Osborne's *A Patriot for Me* just days after hitting town in 1969. It was thanks to a friend, actress (and now head of the National Endowment for the Arts) Jane Alexander, daughter of Harvard's football surgeon, that he was introduced to talent agents in the Big Apple. He then found roles in Sal Mineo's controversial Off-Broadway production of John Herbert's *Fortune and Men's Eyes* (he succeeded the original player in the pivotal role of Rocky, the prison cell-block king) in 1969, Allan Knee's 1972 Civil War drama *Blue Boys* (it lasted a single performance), and others, all of which led him to Joseph Papp's New York Shakespeare Festival. At the Public Theater he acted—still as Tom Lee Jones—in nine plays and later, after establishing himself in films,

would return to the New York stage briefly in Sam Shepard's *True West*.

During his first year or so in New York, Jones married Katherine Lardner, a fellow struggling actor (and later writer) who was the granddaughter of sportswriter Ring Lardner. Following the death of her father, David, while covering the war in Europe for *The New Yorker*, she had been brought up by her uncle, Ring Jr., the screenwriter who later fell victim to Hollywood's blacklist. She had had two children from a previous union. Although the marriage would last a little over seven years, Jones always has been loath to discuss it.

Still using the moniker Tom Lee Jones, he also took a long-running role on television as Dr. Mark Toland in the soap opera *One Life to Live*, playing it on and off from 1971 to 1975, first as an urbane, loving doctor and then, as the part was rewritten after he gave notice of planning to leave, "an A-one nutboy," as he later described it in a 1994 cover story in *Entertainment Weekly*. "Practically over the weekend I went from an upstanding doctor into Mr. Hyde. "They had me kill my parents! About the nicest thing I did was take drugs."

And on Broadway during his Manhattan interlude, Tom Lee Jones had several small roles in the 1971 Sid Caesar–Carol Channing comedy *Four on a Garden*, by Abe Burrows, and played Stephen Dedalus in the 1974 Zero Mostel revival of James Joyce's *Ulysses in Nighttown*, originally done by Mostel Off-Broadway in the late fifties. *New York Post* drama critic Douglas Watt observed: "Tom Lee Jones cuts an appropriately romantic figure as young Dedalus." And Jones also found work in a couple of low-budget films (one made in Canada) that sat around for several years looking for distributors and today are rarely seen.

Working television soaps by day and in the theater by night stymied Tommy Lee. As he told the *New York Times* in 1993, "I was bumping against a ceiling in the theater. I was reasonably well known as a young actor. But Broadway was going through a phase of decay. The plays were getting bigger, broader, less dramatic, and coarser. . . . If I wanted my creative life to grow, the marketplace was telling me I needed to be more famous." So in late 1975 (Tom Lee Jones's last work of the time for Joseph Papp was Michael Weller's *Fishing* in February of that year) he and wife Katherine lit out for Los Angeles, where he could try his luck in films.

His first Hollywood role was in Roger Corman's *Jackson County Jail* (1976), costarring with Yvette Mimieux as two escaped cons on the lam from a rural lockup. Next up: playing a brooding, on-the-edge, man-of-few-words Vietnam vet in the particularly violent *Rolling Thunder* (1977), ready, willing, and able to help his bloodthirsty CO (William Devane) wreak stateside

As Dr. Mark Toland in the heralded *One Life to Live* marriage to Julie Siegel (Lee Warrick)

In *Fishing* for the New York Shakespeare Festival in 1975: the two future Roy Foltriggs from *The Client* by John Grisham—John Heard (who would take the role on TV in 1995) and Tom Lee Jones (who would originate the role on film in 1994). (photo: Friedman-Abeles)

havoc on a bunch of sadists who've maimed the latter and killed his family.

These seemed to have set the not especially ideal pattern for Tommy Lee Jones that persists to the present day—playing second fiddle to the leading lady or playing the scene-stealing screen psychos and nasties. Only on one or two occasions during the next two decades would he carry a film on his own with sole above-the-title billing.

He did some work on such TV series as *Barnaby Jones* and *Baretta,* had a small role in the *Charlie's Angels* TV-movie pilot, and played a motorcycle cop in the disaster TV movie *Smash-up on Interstate 5.* A flashy television role that followed, portraying Howard Hughes in a two-part film about the eccentric billionaire who had died not long before, brought Tommy Lee Jones great acclaim. John O'Connor (*New York Times*) wrote: "Mr. Jones, projecting an uncanny physical resemblance to Hughes, manages the difficult trick of making the character slightly eccentric in his most charming moments, curiously understandable at his most bizzare." The *Village Voice* said: "Tommy Lee Jones is brilliant as Howard Hughes." One critic pointed out that Jones seemed to have come out of nowhere and beat out two hundred other actors, including Warren Beatty, for the plum role. (It seems unlikely that Beatty would have been in the running, since he's never done television after hitting the big time and apparently does not plan to.)

In his third Hollywood film, *The Betsy,* the star-laden 1978 adaptation of Harold Robbins's trashy soap opera with the automobile industry as its setting, Tommy Lee was cast as a hunk-like stud—hardly the image that would drive his career—who beds assorted female cast members and connives his way up the corporate ladder. This was a Laurence Olivier starrer that he did for a lark and the loot, but, hey, how many films are there which have Olivier, then in his seventies, humping his daughter-in-law on-screen?

So it was back to supporting the leading lady—this time Faye Dunaway—in the kinky, enigmatic eye-gouging thriller *Eyes of Laura Mars* (also 1978), which brought him back to New York for filming. In the *New Yorker,* Pauline Kael singled out "an interesting actor named Tommy Lee Jones," and his part as a murderous police lieutenant with a split personality seems to be where most critics "discovered" him. His role as Mooney Lynn, the earthy, nurturing husband and canny manager of country singer Loretta Lynn, in *Coal Miner's Daughter*

As billionaire Howard Hughes . . . young . . . middle-aged . . . and ancient

(1980) cemented his rugged-leading-man status, even though, once again, he supported the star—this time, good Texas buddy Sissy Spacek, who won an Oscar for her performance. Tommy Lee and Sissy later would work together on a couple of other projects, including his directing debut. Of the *Coal Miner's Daughter* role, for which he won a Golden Globe nomination as Best Actor, Jones later mused: "I think this has some of my best work. [Director] Michael Apted let me play Mooney not as a complete jerk but as a man working his way through his problems."

Jones's marriage to Katherine Lardner fell apart in late 1976, and they divorced in 1978. For a brief while, somewhat out of character for one who professes to be a very private man, he was making the Hollywood scene with various starlets on his arm. Ultimately, though, Jones caught the eye of photojournalist and part-time actress Kimberlea Gayle Cloughley, a University of Texas graduate and an extra on *Back Roads*, the movie he was making in Brownsville with Sally Field in mid-1980. Tommy Lee and Kimberlea were married on May 30, 1981, and (as the old bromide goes) became the proud parents of Austin (a.k.a. Bubba), born in 1983, and Victoria (a.k.a. Tory), born in 1991. This second marriage went bust in mid-1995, and such had become Jones's celebrity that the "monumental" splitsville news garnered a two-page spread in *People Weekly*. (Before making *Back Roads*, he starred in an adaptation of William Faulkner's *Barn Burning* for the PBS *American Short Story* series.)

Returning to the New York stage in December 1980 (for the last time to date), Jones costarred with Peter Boyle, playing Austin in Joseph Papp's New York Shakespeare Festival production of Sam Shepard's *True West*. The play lasted a month, and it was then back to television for Tommy Lee, in the role of fast-talking charlatan Bill Starbuck in a new version of *The Rainmaker*, with Tuesday Weld, for director John Frankenheimer. Taped for cable, which then had a rather limited audience, it was not widely seen and has yet to be made available for home video.

This was followed by *The Executioner's Song* (1982) with his astonishing performance as real-life killer Gary Gilmore, the wasted protagonist of Norman Mailer's book of the same title. A two-part television movie that was shown theatrically overseas and has since become an in-demand item on home video, it earned Tommy Lee an Emmy Award as Best Actor for his searing portrait of the convict who chose the road to damnation and then fought a long battle with the state of Utah to be allowed his choice of execution—by firing squad. His animalistic scenes with Rosanna Arquette, his earthy, jail-bait girlfriend, set new standards for network television. (They were both fully clothed for U.S. consumption, but she does a number of her scenes completely undressed in the foreign version and in one of the two available for the domestic home-video market.) Strangely, few latter-day critics noted the similarity in subject—a pair of unbridled lowlifes turned into media superstars at the point of a gun—to Oliver Stone's *Natural Born Killers*, which also had a startling performance by Jones.

In New Zealand in 1982 he then went the Burt Lancaster *Crimson Pirate* route in a swashbuckling romp known in the United States as *Nate and Hayes* but everywhere else as *Savage Islands*. It was the first real "Tommy Lee Jones movie" in that it was his to carry as top-billed star at the head of a cast of lesser American and British names. The film was engaging, as was Jones as colorful, bearded freebooter Bully Hayes. It was beautifully made and action-packed; but it was unable to find an audience.

Jones's performance in *The River Rat*, as a sullen former convict trying to connect with his thirteen-year-old daughter, displayed his remarkable versatility, for the role was a world away from devil-may-care Bully Hayes. The moody film, set on the banks of the Mississippi, was a murder mystery of sorts that had him at a turning point, faced with a tomboy daughter (Martha Plimpton in her screen debut) on the cusp of womanhood and a crooked lawman (nasty Brian Dennehy) dogging him for a hidden cache of stolen loot. No, Jones does not play the title character; it's the name of the broken-down scow he and Plimpton are reconstructing while attempting to establish a rapport.

Back on television in mid-1984, Tommy Lee then played Brick to Jessica Lange's Maggie in a new production of Tennessee Williams's *Cat on a Hot Tin Roof*, made for cable but later shown on PBS's *American Playhouse*. "That would be a good role for me someday," Jones recalled at the time to *USA Today*, noting that he first read the Williams play as a teen. "The language got to me, it was so beautiful." And just in time—Brick, the dissolute, probably homosexual younger son in a crumbling southern aristocratic family, is supposed to be twenty-seven. Jones at the time was thirty-seven. A number of years later, Jones and Lange would rejoin fortuitously in director Tony Richardson's last film, *Blue Sky*.

Television work and moviemaking continued to be interwoven in Jones's resumé, which lengthened with a wide variety of roles. On TV he starred as a disgruntled Vietnam vet who "steals" New York's Central Park in *The Park Is Mine* (1985), holding it for seventy-two hours to make a personal statement about the war, and in *Yuri Nosenko, KGB* (1986) was a dogged CIA agent on the track of a mole, both premiering on HBO. Theatrically, another "Tommy Lee Jones movie" had him playing a freelance thief, botching a government "gig" while get-

In *Eyes of Laura Mars* in 1978 . . .

tation of Larry McMurtry's *Lonesome Dove*, as the dour, white-haired-and-bearded former Texas ranger Woodrow Call on an epic cattle drive with his longtime buddy, bringing him another Emmy nomination as Best Actor.

Jones did another enigmatic loner turn, playing a trained assassin, costarring in *The Package*, a paranoia thriller with Gene Hackman. Though they had only a handful of scenes together, the pair offered moviegoers the opportunity of seeing arguably the two finest players on the contemporary American screen in tandem. *The Package* was the first of Tommy Lee Jones's three (to date) movies with cinematographer-*cum*-director Andrew Davis. In rapid succession, Jones then starred as a dedicated helicopter instructor in Pentagon propaganda called *Fire Birds*, which many saw as a retread of *Top Gun* with Apache choppers in place of screaming jets; played somewhat against type as a sensitive, bespectacled child psychologist in the not-well-received *House of Cards;* and was exceptional as the military officer in a career and marital crisis with Jessica Lange in Tony Richardson's beautiful *Blue Sky*. The last, shot in 1991, was a production for Orion Pictures. That outfit was undergoing severe financial difficulties, and the completed film was shelved before emerging in 1994

. . . and in *The Betsy* the same year

ting involved with a sleek prototype car in a formula action film called *Black Moon Rising*. Then he glowered his way through, and stole the spotlight from colleagues in, *The Big Town*, as a sinister gambling-house owner in fifties Chicago, and the British-made *Stormy Monday*, as a menacing American mobster aiming to take over a working-class town.

Broken Vows, about a conscience-stricken priest who becomes aware of a killer's identity during confession (à la Hitchcock's earlier *I Confess*), and *Stranger on My Land*, dealing with a former Vietnam vet who returns to the family farm, only to have the government try to take it from him for political reasons, gave Jones a couple of strong late-eighties TV roles. These were followed by the noirish, tongue-in-cheek *Gotham,* in which he played a nickel-and-dime private eye who finds himself on the trail of a beautiful dead nympho with whose ghost he has an affair; *April Morning,* from the Howard Fast novel about "the shot heard around the world" on the opening day of the American Revolution, with Texas-drawling Jones—in the days before there was a Texas—somewhat incongruously cast as a British farmer turned Massachusetts colonist who becomes, in effect, the first casualty on Lexington Green; and the sprawling adap-

On the set of *Coal Miner's Daughter* (1980)

and winning an Oscar for Lange. In the meantime, director Richardson had died of AIDS.

Oliver Stone chose Jones to play the relatively small but pivotal role of real-life, white-haired Clay Shaw in *JFK* (1991). The shady New Orleans businessman had close ties to its gay community and to local Castroites and became one of D.A. Jim Garrison's subjects in his obsession with proving that a conspiracy was behind the Kennedy assassination. Jones's menacing figure all but stole the film from its star, Kevin Costner. In the film's climactic courtroom scene, Costner acted his ass off in a lengthy summation as the moviegoer watched the glowering Jones over Costner's shoulder. Tommy Lee earned his first Academy Award nomination as Best Supporting Actor for his performance but lost to Jack Palance in *City Slickers*.

In another film-pilfering role, this time as a maniacal nuclear terrorist, Jones ran rings around star Steven Seagal in Andrew Davis's *Under Siege*, set aboard a U.S. aircraft carrier heading toward Hawaii. Then, also for Davis, Jones had his Oscar-winning role as the relentless, Javert-like U.S. marshal dogging Harrison Ford in *The Fugitive*, one of the most popular and biggest-grossing movies of 1993.

For Oliver Stone, Jones played a "composite figure" American GI in a brief but telling role (though he had top billing as the film's most prominent name) in another of his (Stone's) Vietnam sagas, lengthy *Heaven and Earth*, covering forty years in the life of Vietnamese peasant turned author Le Ly Hayslip (played by film newcomer Hiep Thi Le). Jones doesn't make an appearance until more than halfway through the harrowing tale, does his charismatic thing for about twenty minutes, and then does himself in. Gone, but hardly forgotten—and he even had Texan Debbie Reynolds playing his mom!

Jones's appearance in no less than five films in 1994 (actually four new ones and the long-delayed *Blue Sky*) led more than one critic to joke that he was striving to be in every movie released in the nineties, comparing his seemingly prodigious output to that of Michael Caine in the eighties. In Oliver Stone's *Natural Born Killers* he had a brief but flashy part as the crazed warden who craves the media spotlight that has followed his Bonnie and Clyde prisoners behind his bars; in *Blown Away*, he played a mad IRA bomber with the single-minded mission of vengeance against former buddy Jeff Bridges, and in *The Client*, from John Grisham's bestseller, the egotistical U.S. attorney eager to use a preteen murder

Discussing a scene with director Martin Ritt and costar Sally Field on the set of *Back Roads* (1981)

On his wedding day in May 1981 with bride Kimberlea Cloughley. (photo: Zigy Kaluzny/Gamma Liaison)

witness as a political stepping-stone. (In the last named, costar Susan Sarandon earned an Oscar nomination, giving Tommy Lee the unique distinction of acting opposite two actresses up for Academy Awards in the same year. It was Jessica Lange, of course, who won for *Blue Sky*.) Many critics felt that Tommy Lee Jones's unyielding portrayal of the legendary Ty Cobb, the meanest man in organized baseball, in *Cobb*, rounding out a prolific year on the screen, should have gotten him an Academy Award nomination as Best Actor, but it was not to be.

After finishing *Cobb*, Jones made a well-received directorial debut, starring in (and cowriting) *The Good Old Boys* on cable television. Based on Elmer Kelton's book about a sodbuster and rounder who returns to his West Texas home at the turn of the century, it was cast with a number of Jones's acting buddies, including fellow Texan Sissy Spacek (with whom he worked in both *Coal Miner's Daughter* and *JFK*, though in the latter never in the same scene) and Sam Shepard (the actor-playwright whose earlier *True West* costarred Jones on the New York stage). Both Jones and Spacek received award nominations—he, for a CableAce award as Best Actor; she, for an Emmy as Best Actress.

In his comic-book turn as the colorfully bizarre and patently schizophrenic "Two-Face" in *Batman Forever* in 1995, Jones (second-billed to Val Kilmer's "Batman") had the evil-dripping, now-fueled-with-vengeance role played in the first film in 1989 about the Caped Crusader

As an itinerant con artist, Starbuck, in the 1982 TV version of *The Rainmaker*

Striking a jaunty pose on the New Zealand set of his pirate swashbuckler *Savage Islands* (known in the U.S. as *Nate and Hayes*) in 1983

Jones (with head shaved for *Cobb* filming) with wife, Kimberlea, on Oscar night in 1994

Beaming while holding the Oscar for *The Fugitive* (photo: Academy of Motion Picture Arts and Sciences [AMPAS])

Exuding pure contempt as Clay Shaw at his climactic trial in Oliver Stone's *JFK*

Tommy Lee Jones, cover
subject in 1979 and 1994

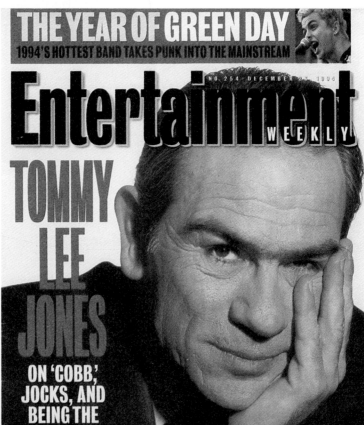

Tommy Lee Jones, cover
subject in 1979 and 1994

The Joneses of the late 1980s

Not long after establishing himself in Hollywood in the late seventies, Tommy Lee Jones told Guy Flatley in *Cosmopolitan,* "I'm proud to be an actor," and revealed, "I don't borrow from other actors. I *steal* whatever and whenever I can, the way all actors do. Acting is a com-

Tommy Lee and Kimberlea Jones with son Austin and daughter Victoria (photo: Demmie Todd)

by Billy Dee Williams as the prescarred Gotham City district attorney Harvey Dent. It even afforded Tommy Lee the unique distinction as an actor of having his visage embossed on glass drinking mugs as a promotional for McDonald's, on cereal boxes for Kellogg's Corn Pops, on Fleer's trading cards, and other products as part of the massive *Batman Forever* exploitation campaign. "There's nobody like Tommy Lee Jones," said director Joel Schumacher, who also worked with him in *The Client.* "I mean, who else can be this wicked, scary, funny, and daring at the same time?"

After seemingly nonstop moviemaking through the first half of the 1990s, there was a lull for Jones and he was off the screen for nearly two full years. Without much publicity, he did manage to make two massive-budget films—one partially on the streets of Manhattan, the other on the streets of Los Angeles. In spring 1996, for executive producer Steven Spielberg, he began the sci-fi alien comedy *Men in Black.* And while that one was in lengthy postproduction to get all the special effects right, Jones then proceeded on to the disaster movie, *Volcano.* The two ultimately went into release in late spring/early summer 1997 in reverse order. A reprise of his indefatigable *Fugitive* lawman character in *U.S. Marshals* was next on his filming agenda. And there were reports that he was preparing to make his big-screen directorial debut after that with *3rd Down and Forever,* about the real-life Joe Don Looney, an early-sixties college football star who went on to an abortive pro career, Vietnam duty, and years of meditation with an Indian guru before becoming the victim of a motorcycle accident at forty-five. Jones would be playing a supporting role as Looney's dad.

In his only priest role, in TV's *Broken Vows* (1987)

In his portrayal of baseball great Tyrus Raymond Cobb in 1994 (photo: Sidney Baldwin)

On the set of TV's *The Good Old Boys* in mid-1994 in his directorial mode (photo: Erik Heinila)

munal profession; we contribute to one another." Now well into his career as a major good guy–bad guy name, both as a charismatic screen menace and a performer who has perfected thinking-man leads, Jones—like the Jack Nicholsons and the Robert De Niros—can probably relish seeing other younger actors stealing from him.

Tommy Lee, who today augments his daytime job salary doing commercial voice-overs for Red Dog Beer, maintains this philosophy about his profession: "People who will suggest that the American motion-picture audience is dumb are sadly mistaken. Americans are not dumb. We don't read enough books; we may watch too much television. But these people are not idiots. So that's why I say that even if you're not dealing with a formula situation—formula story, formula plot—you have a responsibility to make it new and different and stimulating."

THE FILMS

LOVE STORY (1970): Tom Lee Jones gloats over a winning hand as college roommate Ryan O'Neal (*center*) comes into their dorm room following a terrific date.

1

LOVE STORY

PARAMOUNT PICTURES, 1970

CAST

Ali MacGraw (*Jenny Cavilleri*), Ryan O'Neal (*Oliver Barrett IV*), Ray Milland (*Oliver Barrett III*), John Marley (*Phil Cavilleri*), Katherine Balfour (*Mrs. Oliver Barrett III*), Russell Nype (*Dean Thompson*), Sydney Walker (*Dr. Shapely*), Robert Modica (*Dr. Addison*), Walker Daniels (*Ray Stratton*), Tom Lee Jones (*Hank*), John Merensky (*Steve*), Andrew Duncan (*Reverend Blauvelt*), Bob O'Connell (*Tommy the Doorman*).

CREDITS

A Howard G. Minsky–Arthur Hiller production. *Executive producer,* David Golden; *producer,* Howard G. Minsky; *director,* Arthur Hiller; *screenplay,* Erich Segal; *cinematographer,* Dick Kratina; *art director,* Robert Gundlach; *music,* Francis Lai; *editor,* Robert C. Jones. In color; *running time,* 100 minutes.

The once-and-always "Love means never having to say you're sorry" movie, which emerged as one of the most popular romantic flicks of its day, began life as a screenplay by Erich Segal, who then turned his script into a novel that became an instant bestseller. It was published before the release of the film, which was shot primarily in and around Harvard in Cambridge, Massachusetts, and in New York City. Overnight the four-hankie weeper

Jones in the second of his two scenes in the incredibly popular Arthur Hiller film.

made screen stars of Ryan O'Neal, playing a wealthy Harvard law student, and Ali MacGraw, a snooty Radcliffe junior from a working-class background. They meet, romance, bicker, romp in the snow, argue over hockey, fall in love, and marry. "Preppie" O'Neal insists on making it on his own and turns his back on the family fortunes and his distant but filthy-rich father (Ray Milland, surprising audiences of the time in his film comeback without the fantastic toupee he had worn throughout his leading-man days).

Things go swimmingly for the young lovebirds once they hit Manhattan. O'Neal gets a fabulous job in a prestigious law firm, and they move into Park Avenue digs. Then MacGraw falls ill. (The affliction became known to movie fans of the day as the "Ali MacGraw disease," since it was never quite identified in the film.) O'Neal swallows his pride and goes to his father for money but is reticent to tell him why. Dad writes him a check but would like a reconciliation and an "I love you" from his son. He gets neither. The teary climax to the film, set against the incessant but popular main theme of Francis Lai's music, apparently affected millions of moviegoers of the time, judging from *Love Story*'s huge box-office success. The picture earned stardom for both O'Neal and MacGraw, more fleetingly for her than him. (O'Neal

31

went on to do an ill-advised sequel weeper in 1978 called *Oliver's Story*, with Candice Bergen as his leading lady.)

The focus of *Love Story* remained firmly on the two attractive leads, but working on the periphery was a recent Harvard cum laude graduate named Tom Lee Jones. He had two brief scenes as one of lovelorn O'Neal's roommates but not much of an opportunity to make an impression one way or the other. Ironically, Jones's career eclipsed those of the film's stars.

2

ELIZA'S HOROSCOPE

O-ZALI FILMS, 1970 (*released only in Canada in 1975*)

CAST

Elizabeth Moorman (*Eliza*), Tom Lee Jones (*Tommy*), Lila Kedrova (*Lila*), Rose Quong (*Chinese astrologer*), Richard Manuel (*Bearded composer*), Pierre Bryand (*Clown and harmonica boy*), Marcel Sabourin (*Pervert doctor*), Therese Curotte (*Tom's grandmother*), Alanis Obomsawin (*Indian maiden*), Chester Goodleaf, Kevin Horn, Donald Phillips (*Indians*), Denis Lacroix (*Watching Indian*), Claude Gai (*Silas*), Michael Mailhot (*Blip*), Chiitra Neogy (*Baptismal man*), Nicole Garon (*Whipped nun*), Fred Waterhouse (*Crazy Frank*), Angelyne Tremblay (*Pregnant woman*), Roy Alexander (*Nimbo*), Tamara Cardinal (*Stripper*), François Barbeau (*Winter tramp*), Jacques Normand (*Cemetery bishop*).

CREDITS

An O-Zali production. *Producer-director-writer-editor,* Gordon Sheppard; *cinematographers,* Jean Boffety, Paul Van Der Linden, Michael Brault; *art director/costumes,* François Barbeau; *music,* Elmo Peeler. In color; *running time,* 120 minutes.

Jones (he was still Tom Lee) made his second film appearance in a key role in this infrequently seen movie that, according to *Variety,* was in the editing stage for four years. Reviewing it at the Stratford Ontario International Film Festival in September 1975, the pa-

per's critic called *Eliza's Horoscope* "one of the most astonishing, enigmatic feature films ever to come out of Canada. . . . Superficially, but only so, it bears some resemblance to Fellini's *Juliet of the Spirits* in its theme of a young girl desperately seeking to make her fortune come true."

This obscure film, coming at the tail end of the drugged-out sixties (the residue of which permeates the whole thing), seems to have had only sporadic release outside Canada. It deals with the quest of a waiflike free spirit named Eliza for the perfect astrological mate—preferably a rich one—to father her child. "I'm looking, looking for love," she sings to herself as she skips through the back streets of Montreal. "I think the stars know who my love is." Her search for a rich husband is instigated by an elderly Chinese woman who has charted her course. (Rose Quong, then ninety-one, a venerable Australian-born actress of the Chinese theater, came out of retirement for the role.) Eliza rooms with a blowsy middle-aged hooker (Lila Kedrova) in an apartment building inhabited by poor Indian males while conducting her often bizarre odyssey and takes up with an enigmatic lover, played by Tom Lee Jones.

While Eliza is following her search that leads her to an orgiastic banker's convention, a graveyard (the would-be "man of her dreams" she meets there turns out to be a priest), and a yachtsman with a strange sexual fetish, Tom, the Canadian Indian steelworker, is pursuing his

ELIZA'S HOROSCOPE (1970): With his lover, played by Elizabeth Moorman, in the obscure Canadian film made in 1970 but not released for a number of years . . .

. . . and with Lila Kedrova, the middle-aged madam

Jones, in a rare show of delight, as the enigmatic Canadian-Indian bridge builder.

Doing his first screen nude scene, being ministered to by Elizabeth Moorman

own particular dream—to bomb a bridge as a statement against injustice to his people. "Look at that mother," Tom tells Eliza during one of the film's more comprehensible moments, when they both come upon the bridge on which he has destructive designs. "They had to use Indian labor, too. My father worked on that bridge. I'll tell you what. I'm gonna work on it, too." As Eliza sinks further into a hallucinatory haze, Tom and his Indian pals make a disastrous raid on the bridge, and he ends up being shot. A message he leaves on a piece of birch bark is delivered to Eliza: "Waited as long as I could. See you in the sun. Tom." It finally dawns on Eliza who he was—her ideal man—and she packs her bags and moves on to continue her search in another city.

Between the Felliniesque aspects, the grotesque, dreamlike sequences involving sadism and rape, the writer-director's fascination with the mystical, and the relatively lucid portions involving Eliza's relationship with Tom and his bomb-making mission, *Eliza's Horoscope* emerged as bold, experimental filmmaking of the sort in which Oliver Stone would dabble two decades later in *Natural Born Killers*—in which, coincidentally, a more seasoned Tommy Lee Jones would also appear. "But what [Gordon Sheppard] is trying to say and achieve is not discernible," *Variety* wrote. "The acting is weak, and the film, for all its colorful sequences of dreams, flashbacks and one kind of reality, is a failure." On the other hand, the *Los Angeles Times* considered it "a boldly assertive and original work . . . a remarkable piece of filmmaking by any standard."

Eliza's Horoscope, shot in 1970 over fifteen weeks and edited in a four-to-five year marathon, initially was to have been distributed by Warner Bros., but the studio backed out of the project after seeing rushes and the escalating budget. Gordon Sheppard's "Xanadu," as the film magazine *Take One* called it, premiered in May 1975 at the Unitarian Church in Montreal. (It had a single preview showing in New York in November of that year at the Elgin Theater and ultimately surfaced on home video a decade later.) *Eliza's Horoscope* was the winner of five Canadian film awards, including Best Supporting Actress (Lila Kedrova), cinematography, and art direction, and director Sheppard was given the "Auteur" Award. It was also the Gold Medal winner at the Festival of the Americas.

3

LIFE STUDY

NEBBCO PRODUCTIONS, 1973

CAST

Bartholomew Miro Jr. (*Angelo Corelli*), Erika Peterson (*Myrna Clement*), Ziska (*The model*), Gregory D'Alessio (*Adrian Clement*), Tom Lee Jones (*Gus*), Rosetta Garufi (*Grandma*), Anthony Forest (*John Clement*), Yvonne Sherwell (*Peggy Clement*), Emmett Priest (*Jim Rowe*), Ed Mona (*Vinnie*), John Toland (*Ken Lambert*), Fritz Kopell (*Helen Hopkinson*), Priscilla Bardonville (*Veda*), Lynette Dupret (*Angelo's mother*), John Feeney (*Joe Levine*), Candy Latson (*Frank Walker*), Bob Roberts (*Angelo's father*), Efigenio Miha (*Pedro*), Max Anderson (*Father Gunnarson*), David Hendricks (*First hood*), Gregory Heinlin (*Second hood*), Anthony John (*Angelo as a boy*)

CREDITS

Executive producer, Stephen Hochhauser; *producer-director-cinematographer,* Michael Nebbia; *screenplay,* Arthur Birnkrant, *based on a story by* Nebbia; *music,* Emmanuel Vardi; *editors,* Ray Sandiford and Sidney Katz. DeLuxe color; *running time,* 99 minutes.

A plain-Jane teenager, newly pregnant, who chases and eventually wins a young Greenwich Village filmmaker from the coal mines of West Virginia is the heroine of this flamboyant, often whimsical, but low-budget, little-seen romance with Freudian, religious, and ecological under-tones. The hero, unfortunately, was written and acted as sullen and humorless. Tom Lee Jones (he was Tom Lee here for the last time) gave a hint of his later charisma as the hero's sanitation-collector buddy and was the only member of the no-name cast to go on to better things.

Life Study, filmed in June 1970 in Middletown, New York, and Dembo and Pittsburgh, Pennsylvania, was directed by Michael Nebbia, whose only other claim to fame appears to be having been cinematographer on *Alice's Restaurant.* Belatedly, in 1973, the film received a one-week showcase in Manhattan at a popular "in" art movie house of the time called the First Avenue Screening Room before effectively vanishing from sight. But before it did, Vincent Canby caught up with it and, telescoping the sparse plot into three sentences, wrote in his *New York Times* review "The way is thus immediately prepared for a film that attempts to honor squareness but ends up by demonstrating it. . . . Bartholomew Miro Jr. plays Angelo, Erika Peterson is Myrna, and a girl named Ziska is the worldly model who represents the flesh opposed to Myrna's spirit. I haven't the faintest idea if any of them can act." Canby also felt that the film was "neither good enough nor strong enough to compete in the commercial market. However, it is the first [and, as it turns out, the only] directorial effort of [Michael] Nebbia, whose talent as a cinematographer should earn him the right to fail publicly as a director."

Life Study apparently has never been available on video. The prime interest of this exceedingly low budget film remains young Tommy Lee Jones, who was doing the New York stage scene and some live television at the time. Just prior to working in this movie, he was starring Off-Broadway as Rocky, the brutish jailhouse rapist in Sal Mineo's production of the notorious, gay-themed *Fortune and Men's Eyes,* having replaced Bartholomew Miro Jr., the lead in *Life Study.*

LIFE STUDY (1973): Tom Lee Jones in his least seen film, made during his days as a New York actor, shown briefly several years after being made and then vanishing, presumably forever.

Yvette Mimieux, Jones's first Hollywood leading lady, before being put through jailhouse indignities

4

JACKSON COUNTY JAIL

NEW WORLD PICTURES, 1976

CAST

Yvette Mimieux (*Dinah Hunter*), Tommy Lee Jones (*Coley Blake*), Robert Carradine (*Bobby Ray*), Frederic Cook (*Hobie*), Severn Darden (*Sheriff Dempsey*), Howard Hesseman (*David*), John Lawlor (*Deputy Burt*), Britt Leach (*Bartender Dan Oldum*), Nan Martin (*Allison*), Nancy Noble (*Lola*), Lisa Copeland (*Girl in commercial*), Clifford Emmich (*Mr. Bigelow*), Michael Ashe (*Mr. Cooper*), Edward Marshall (*Mr. Blight*), Marcie Drake (*Candy, David's girl-friend*), Betty Thomas (*Waitress*), Ken Lawrence (*Paulie*), Arthur Wong (*Cook*), Marci Barkin (*Girl in restaurant*), Michael Hikene (*Vincent Lepardo*), Roy David Hagle (*Ambulance driver*), William Molloy (*Deputy Lyle Peters*), Ira Miller (*Drunk man*), Jackie Robin (*Drunk woman*), Gus Peters (*Melon Man Shaw*), Patrice Rohmer (*Cassie Anne*), Amparo Mimieux (*Poquita*), Mary Woronov (*Pearl*), Hal Needham (*Chief of Fallsburg Police*), and Richard Lockmiller, Jack O'Leary, Duffy Hambleton, Mark Carlton, Don Hinz, James Arnett, Norma Moye.

CREDITS

Executive producer, Roger Corman; *producer,* Jeff Begun; *director,* Michael Miller; *screenplay,* Donald Stewart; *cinematographer,* Bruce Logan; *art director,* Michael McCloskey; *music,* Loren Newkirk; *editor,* Caroline Ferriol. Metrocolor; running time, 84 minutes.

Tommy Lee Jones's first significant feature film, a noirish low-rent road picture produced with grit by Roger Corman, found him as a sullen prisoner in a small-town southern jail. Into it a fashionable but battered former advertising executive from Los Angeles (Yvette Mimieux), having dumped her job and her cheating boyfriend and lit out for New York by car, has been tossed after having been picked up on charges of theft. Her story: having been car-jacked at gunpoint by a pill-popping couple (Robert Carradine and Nancy Noble), to whom she has given a lift, she'd been left by the side of the road unconscious without any identification. Finding herself in nightmare land, she had staggered to a roadhouse, where she was assaulted by the drunken bartender, who then tells the cops she tried to hold him up.

In the pokey that night she is viciously raped by jailer Frederic Cook, whom she hysterically clubs to death with a stool. The bad dude in the adjoining cell is Tommy Lee Jones, a truck hijacker and killer cynical to the core, who helps her escape, persuading her that she has no chance if she stays to explain the murder. To him, life sucks. "I'm a thief because I want to be a thief," he tells her. "I don't wanna be nothin' else. Nothin' wrong with bein' a crook. Everybody's crooked. I never met a straight person in my whole life. The whole damn country is a rip-off—and everybody in it." This is, as one critic pointed out, a road picture about the total disintegration of bourgeois America in its bicentennial year.

With the law on their tail, the fugitives spend the night at an abandoned farmhouse. There Jones tries to convince Mimieux that her situation forces her to "drop out and go under." Mimieux and Jones, who was facing life imprisonment before getting the chance to flee ("I'll play what's dealt," he tells her), make their way into the town of Fallsburg, with the cops closing in and a local Bicentennial parade interrupting their path. "They're gonna kill you!" she screams at him. "I don't mind," he responds calmly. "I was born dead." Ambushed, she is wounded and subsequently captured, and he is shot to death in a memorable set piece as the parade passes by (although why the police would engage in a deadly shoot-out in the middle of the marchers, with the entire town lining the street, is incomprehensible). He collapses on top of an American flag lying across a stop sign painted on the road.

In *Film Comment*, director Michael Miller observed: "If I did a sequel, I'd always want Tommy Lee Jones to be in it, but playing the antithesis from the first film. A cop. So in Part Two, Yvette would again come up with a hard type who would tell the other side of the same story, in just as romantic terms. Then cut it all together some time. We'd have had this wonderfully absurdist movie where our hero plays his own antithesis. But I couldn't get Tommy Lee. . . .Tommy Lee in *Jackson County* is a cliché—I shot him the way John Ford would have. The rape is also a cliché, but I also really think it's the best rape on film." Jones himself later ruminated on his part while chatting with show-business writer Bernard Weintraub of the *New York Times:* "It was the Roger Corman hero. Film-noir hero. Dead on arrival. Man without a country. On the lam. Fast pickup. Pretty girl. Big pistol. A lot of fun along the way. It was a neat little film."

Critic Archer Winsten (*New York Post*) found that the

JACKSON COUNTY JAIL (1976): Surly prisoner Tommy Lee being questioned by Severn Darden, as the redneck sheriff, as his deputy (William Molloy) looks on

The escapees in a rare moment of reflection before the law closes in again

On the lam with fellow prisoner Yvette Mimieux, having just killed a stranger who might have turned them in.

41

Shooting it out with
pursuers in the film's
final minutes

movie had "a quality that lifts it above its class. . . . Partly, no doubt, it is the superior performance of Yvette Mimieux in the star role. It might also be that a newcomer, Tommy Lee Jones, sporting backgrounds as disparate as Texas, football and Harvard, is also impressive as Coley Blake, a criminal by choice." Kevin Thomas, writing in the *Los Angeles Times,* found the film "loaded with surprises . . . a harrowing image of Bicentennial America that doesn't just touch a contemporary raw nerve here and there but a complex nerve of sensibilities. . . ."

Jackson County Jail (called by the *New York Times*'s Vincent Canby "film making of relentless energy and harrowing excitement") became a surprise success and a cult item, of sorts, and Michael Miller, feeling he hadn't gotten it quite right the first time around, reworked the

initial premise two years later as a television movie called *Outside Chance.* Yvette Mimieux reprised her role, and a number of the same actors and production people were involved again. In this version, everything was as it was in the original up to the time she kills the jailer who has assaulted her. The prisoner in the next cell (the Tommy Lee Jones role without Tommy Lee Jones), who has witnessed her plight, urges her to run, but she decides to remain in her cell and take her chances with the law. In this version of the story, she befriends a couple of female cellmates, an accused murderess and a pyromaniac, and learns that one of the hitchhikers who could prove her innocence is also serving time in Jackson County Jail, but her chance to vindicate herself literally goes up in flames.

The famous climactic scene that has Jones encountering a
dead end at the head of a local Bicentennial parade

5

ROLLING THUNDER

AMERICAN INTERNATIONAL, 1977

CAST

William Devane (*Maj. Charles Rane*), Tommy Lee Jones (*Sgt. Johnny Vohden*), Linda Haynes (*Linda Forchet*), James Best (*Texan*), Dabney Coleman (*Maxwell*), Lisa Richards (*Janet Rane*), Luke Askew (*Automatic Slim*), Lawrason Driscoll (*Clif*), James Victor (*Lopez*), Cassie Yates (*Candy*), Jordan Gerler (*Mark Rane*), Jane Abbott (*Sister*), Jerry Brown (*First patrolman*), Jacques Burandt (*Bebe*), Anthony Castillo (*Street urchin*), Charles Escamilla (*T Bird*), Randy Herman (*Billy Sanchez*), and Robert K. Guthrie, Ray Gutierrez, James N. Harrell, Michael Nakamura, Pete Ortega, Paul A. Partian, James Conner Pribble, Cheyenne Rivera, Carol Sava, Robert Raymond Reves, Arturo R. Tamez Jr., Bob Tisdale, Autry Ward, Wert Ward, William Vance Witte, Michael R. White, Alan Wong.

CREDITS

Executive producer, Lawrence Gordon; *producer,* Norman T. Herman; *director,* John Flynn; *screenplay,* Paul Schrader and Heywood Gould, *from a story by* Schrader; *cinematographer,* Jordan Cronenweth; *art director,* Steve Berger; *music,* Barry DeVorzon; *editor,* Frank P. Keller. Color by Deluxe; *running time,* 99 minutes.

Returning to his hometown of San Antonio with a taciturn fellow vet (Tommy Lee Jones) after eight years in a Viet Cong prison camp, tough William Devane, as deco-rated officer Charlie Rane, has found a hero's welcome, a wife who wants a divorce, and a young son who doesn't know him. He soon is presented with a spanking new Cadillac and a couple of thousand silver dollars, one for each day of his confinement—accepting them just as impassively as he has accepted the news that his wife has been cheating on him. As written by Paul Schrader, a year after his *Taxi Driver* hit the screen, it presents his leading character as a tightly wound, compli-cated, tough-as-nails figure that sooner rather than later will explode. The explosion comes when a gang of thugs break into Charlie's home in search of his silver dollars. Knowing his secret for survival, they torture him for the money, grinding his right hand in a garbage disposal, kill his wife and son, and leave him for dead. (The contro-versial, graphic hand-grinding scene was substantially modified reportedly after audience protest at a preview.)

Whereas he had been strangely subdued before the brutal attack, Charlie becomes icy and sets out to mete out his own jungle-warfare justice after being fitted with a hook to replace his mangled hand. Brooding, a walk-ing dead man, he begins his *Death Wish*–like trail of vengeance, enlisting the help of the equally icy Tommy Lee Jones, a trancelike Vietnam buddy with his own demons bottled up inside, and loving Linda Haynes, a shopworn barmaid who wore his bracelet while he was a POW and is looking for romance. There's a jingoistic scene in which Jones, the former sergeant, apologizes to

As Sgt. John Vohden, stateside but not ecstatic

Devane, the former major, for the fact that his family prefers Japanese cars over American ones. (One can imagine the film being remade two decades later with Jones and Devane swapping roles.) In one sleazy bar after another on the Mexican border, with his hook now ground to razor sharpness, he and his two companions (she's along as a decoy) use strong-arm methods to keep information coming in about the four thugs who maimed him. The sadistic four are joined by about a dozen hardened associates. Seemingly emotionless Devane and no-nonsense Jones, filled with a quiet, lethal determination and fearless as only those can be who already consider themselves dead men, are led in full uniform and sawed-off guns to a border brothel in pursuit of instant and massive retaliation. The climactic bloodbath is staged in a combat attack with an arsenal of military weapons.

Despite his billing, Jones, as Devane's loyal buddy suffering the same Vietnam traumas, has only a few scenes. He's in the opening one as the two fly into San Antonio but then disappears (to El Paso) for a long stretch. He is next seen in a vet rehab hospital looking after Devane following a murderous attack on the latter. Ultimately, the two get together at Jones's home. There they hatch a plan to go after the bad guys and then join for the bordertown assault, where Jones, having had no more than a dozen lines in the entire film, almost gleefully tells the whore (a nude Cassie Yates) servicing him, "Gotta go! I'm gonna kill a bunch o' people," zipping up his pants and snapping together an AK-47 as a maniacal glint materializes in his eye and a faint leer crosses his lips.

Molly Haskell (*New York*) found the work "one of the most unapologetically violent films to come along in quite a while. . . . Devane plays a major who spent seven years in a Viet Cong prison and has been tortured into a state of numbness reminiscent of that other Schrader catatonic, *Taxi Driver*'s Travis Bickle (the screenplay to *Rolling Thunder* was written in 1973 before he tackled the De Niro movie). . . . The men—Devane and his fellow catatonic veteran, Tommy Lee Jones—come off better than the women because they are excused from ever uttering a word." In her *New York Post* review of the ultraviolent revenge drama, then critic Judith Crist observed: "*Rolling Thunder* is an infuriating film. It has so many good things about it for starters that its sudden and then total deterioration makes you want to lynch the projectionist."

The *New York Times*'s Vincent Canby, who also compared the Devane role of Charlie to De Niro's Travis Bickle, said this of relative newcomer Tommy Lee Jones: "[He] effectively suggests a man who, though he pretends to be like anyone else, now lives in a small closet in the back of his soul. Like Charlie, he is haunted but ever alert—and armed to the teeth." In Britain's *Monthly Film Bulletin*, reviewer Tom Milne noted: "Contrived in the extreme—had the intruders done the logical thing and killed Rane as well as his family, there wouldn't have been any film—it seems to have little aim, and certainly no effect, other than titillation."

Rolling Thunder had an uncertain history. The "schizophrenic movie" (Judith Crist's words) initially was to go into production in 1975, with writer Paul Schrader making his directing debut. Producer Lawrence Gordon had difficulty obtaining funding for a work that a number of Hollywood studios felt was unconscionably bloody. Schrader turned his script over to another director, John Flynn, who had made the Robert Ryan mob melodrama *The Outfit*, and *Rolling Thunder* was completed in early 1976 as an independent production optioned by Sam Arkoff for American International Pictures. It then popped up on the Columbia Pictures schedule, then on Twentieth Century Fox's, before ultimately falling back into American International's hands.

Engaging the services of a local prostitute (Cassie Yates) before embarking on the film's bloodbath . . .

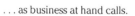

. . . as business at hand calls.

6

THE BETSY

HAROLD ROBBINS INTERNATIONAL/
ALLIED ARTISTS, 1978

CAST

Laurence Olivier (*Loren Hardeman Sr., "Number One"*),
Robert Duvall (*Loren Hardeman III*), Katharine Ross (*Sally
Hardeman*), Tommy Lee Jones (*Angelo Perino*), Jane
Alexander (*Alicia Hardeman*), Lesley-Anne Down (*Lady
Roberta Ayres*), Joseph Wiseman (*Jake Weinstein*),
Kathleen Beller (*Betsy Hardeman*), Edward Herrmann (*Dan
Weyman*), Paul Rudd (*Loren Hardeman Jr.*), Roy Poole
(*John Duncan*), Richard Venture (*Mark Sampson*), Titos
Vandis (*Angelo Luigi Perino*), Clifford David (*Joe Warren*),
Inga Swenson (*Mrs. Craddock*), Whitney Blake (*Elizabeth
Hardeman*), Carol Willard (*Roxanne*), Read Morgan
(*Donald*), Charlie Fields (*Loren III as a boy*), and Robert
Phalen, Nick Czmyr, Norman Palmer, Fred Carney, Maury
Cooper, Russell Porter, Teri Ralston, Warney H. Ruhl,
Patrick J. Monks, William Roerick, William B. Cain, Edward
C. Higgins, Mary Petrie, H. August Kuehl, Robert Hawkins,
Sadie Hawkins, Anthony Steere.

CREDITS

An Emanuel L. Wolf production. *Producer,* Robert R.
Weston; *associate producer,* Jack Grossberg; *director,* Daniel
Petrie; *screenplay,* Walter Bernstein and William Bast; *based
on the novel by* Harold Robbins; *cinematographer,* Mario
Tosi; *production designer,* Herman A. Blumenthal; *music,*
John Barry; *editor,* Rita Roland. Technicolor; *running time,*
125 minutes.

In this stellar, garish potboiler of Harold Robbins's trashy
novel about the multigenerational travails of an automotive tycoon and his family and associates, Tommy Lee
Jones plays what contemporary soap opera fans would
call "the resident hunk," favoring three-piece suits and
occasionally stripping to the waist and beyond. He portrays a daredevil Italian race-car driver (with a Texas
twang) who seizes the opportunity offered him by tycoon Laurence Olivier to build a revolutionary new
model; to bed Kathleen Beller, the great granddaughter
of the old man (called by all including his progeny
"Number One"); to insinuate his way past Number One's
officious, philandering grandson (Robert Duvall), who is
technically his boss and wants to scuttle the car project;
to have an affair with the latter's mistress; and ultimately
to try for a leveraged buyout of the company.

Jones is first seen being wiped out on the track in a
championship race, limping away from the wreck, and
soon being approached by retired Detroit nabob Olivier
to come work for him and put his car-designing expertise
to work on a visionary automobile. Living high on the
hog, seducing and being seduced by the beautiful people who populate pulp fiction by Harold Robbins,
Danielle Steel, Sidney Sheldon, Jacqueline Susann, et
al., Jones, as hot-blooded but oh, so smooth Angelo
Perino, glides through the proceedings and, as *Variety*
observed, "plays his role with a mixture of edginess and
offhandedness—a combination of Burt Reynolds and

The
Harold Robbins
people.
What you desire
…they dare.
What you dream
…*they do!*

HAROLD
ROBBINS'
The Betsy

EMANUEL L. WOLF Presents
LAURENCE OLIVIER

ROBERT DUVALL KATHARINE ROSS TOMMY LEE JONES JANE ALEXANDER in HAROLD ROBBINS' THE BETSY LESLEY-ANNE DOWN JOSEPH WISEMAN
EDWARD HERRMANN PAUL RUDD KATHLEEN BELLER Screenplay by WILLIAM BAST and WALTER BERNSTEIN Music JOHN BARRY
R | RESTRICTED   Produced by ROBERT R. WESTON Directed by DANIEL PETRIE An Allied Artists/Harold Robbins International Production An Allied Artists Release
© 1978 Allied Artists Pictures Corp.

Harvey Keitel. His style—it's got a sense of humor and a campy quality to it—seems more to the point. It's almost trashy."

Amid the goings-on, which one writer said came down to four main interests—cars, sex, money, and power—the tale, when not preoccupied with boardrooms or bedrooms, comes to its own climax, of sorts, when Jones (or Perino), having become increasingly ruthless and obsessed with winning, manages to acquire enough of the family stock shares and, with the four percent given him earlier by Number One, threatens to take control of the company after ousting nemesis Duvall. All of this after Number One has reluctantly decided to drop the car project after being vilified in the automotive press. "We can fight this magazine," Jones insists to the old man. "We'll

mount a nationwide magazine campaign of our own. We'll go to Nader, we'll go to the guys in *Consumer Reports*, we'll show the car performing on television to the entire world. We can do it. It can be done. I can do it!" But Number One is unconvinced and knows when to fold. "When the board meets next week, I'm votin' to drop the Betsy."

Only at the fade-out does Perino find out that he has been outfoxed by his mentor, the old fox himself. Number One has called in long-standing markers, including those from Perino's grandfather, who may or may not have given him mob money to purchase the shares from Duvall's unhappy wife (Jane Alexander) and from the adoring Beller, after whom the revolutionary car is named. As the smirk fades from his face, as he

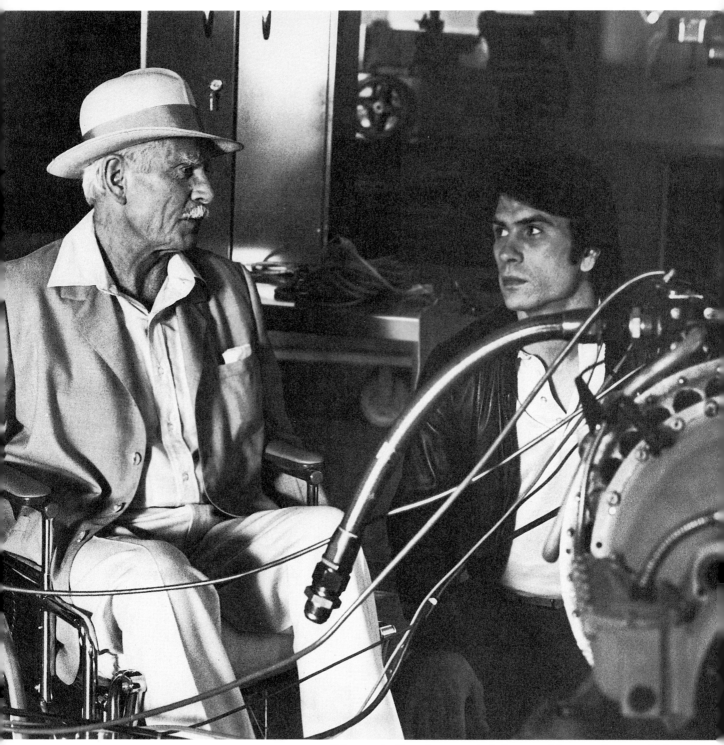

Being recruited from the racetrack pits by automobile tycoon Laurence Olivier . . .

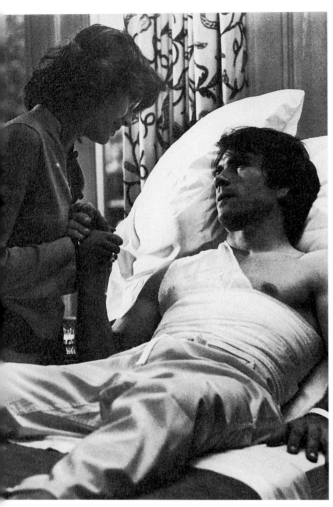

... being comforted by Katharine Ross after a speedway crackup ...

Harold Robbins requires. . . . When the actresses are stripped for their carnal numbers, you're embarrassed— not because they're nude but because they're nude and it isn't risqué, it isn't bawdy, it isn't titillating. They've taken off their clothes for nothing."

... and later being seduced by high-born Lesley-Anne Down

sees his dreams of power in the extravagant corner office quickly evaporating, he hesitantly asks Olivier, having gained back that old unscrupulousness that had made him his millions forty years earlier, who is walking out the office door, "What do I do when you're gone?" To which Number One, turning back to him ever so briefly, responds in his quasi–Scottish-Midwestern accent, "Oh, yeah . . . better learn fast!"

In his *Newsweek* review, critic Jack Kroll, like his fellow reviewers, scoffed at the risable enterprise and ended by noting that "Aside from Olivier's virtuoso performance, the only extraordinary items in *The Betsy* are young Kathleen Beller's beautiful nude scene and young Tommy Lee Jones, a mysteriously 'hot' newcomer with an awesome inability to register a single recognizable human emotion." Pauline Kael, at the time doyenne among the major critics, scoffed in *The New Yorker*, ignoring all but Olivier: ". . . it's tranquil trash. [Daniel] Petrie doesn't have the juicy vulgarity of soul which

At right, as an interloper in a family photo, that includes (*from left*) Robert Duvall, Edward
Herrmann, Leslie-Anne Down, Paul Rudd, Kathleen Beller, Joseph Wiseman, Inga Stevens,
Titos Vandis, and (*in front*) Jane Alexander, Laurence Olivier, and Katharine Ross

Ex–race driver Jones being given the tour of the plant by auto exec Edward Herrmann

With tycoon Olivier's granddaughter, Kathleen Beller, the namesake of the title car

7

EYES OF LAURA MARS

COLUMBIA PICTURES, 1978

CAST

Faye Dunaway (*Laura Mars*), Tommy Lee Jones (*John Neville*), Brad Dourif (*Tommy Ludlow*), René Auberjonois (*Donald Phelps*), Raul Julia (*Michael Reisler*), Frank Adonis (*Sal Volpe*), Lisa Taylor (*Michele*), Darlanne Fluegel (*Lulu*), Rose Gregorio (*Elaine Cassell*), Bill Boggs (*Himself*), Steve Marachuk (*Robert*), Meg Mundy (*Doris Spenser*), Marilyn Meyers (*Sheila Weissman*), Michael Tucker (*Bert*), and Gary Bayer, Mitchell Edmonds, Jeff Niki, Toshi Matsuo, John E. Allen, Anna Anderson, Deborah Beck, Jim Devine, Hanny Friedman, Winnie Hollman, Patty Oja, Donna Palmer, Sterling St. Jacques, Rita Tellone, Kari Page, Dallas Edward Hayes, John Randolph Jones, Al Joseph, Gerald Kline, Sal Richards, Tom Degidon, Paula Lawrence, Joey R. Mills, John Sahag, Hector Troy.

CREDITS

Executive producer, Jack H. Harris; *producer,* Jon Peters; *associate producer,* Laura Ziskin; *director,* Irvin Kershner; *screenplay,* John Carpenter and David Zelag Goodman, *from a story by* Carpenter; *cinematographer,* Victor J. Kemper; *production designer,* Gene Callahan; *art director,* Robert Gundlach; *"Eyes of Laura Mars" photographs,* Rebecca Blake; *music,* Artie Kane; *song "Prisoner" by* John Desautels and Karen Lawrence, *performed by* Barbra Streisand; *costumes,* Theoni V. Aldredge; *editor,* Michael Kahn. Metrocolor; *Running time,* 103 minutes.

EYES OF LAURA MARS (1978): His first encounter with Faye Dunaway, looking into the eyes of Laura Mars at her chi-chi gallery show

In this stylish thriller, a voyeuristic whodunit cowritten by John Carpenter (who hadn't yet hit it big with *Halloween*) and David Zelag Goodman, Faye Dunaway is a chic New York fashion photographer blessed—or cursed—with visions, and Tommy Lee Jones is a police lieutenant investigating a series of murders about which she has had accurate premonitions. Laura Mars, renowned for her controversial, titillating, often kinky photos that frequently depict violent death, actually has the ability to "see" through the eyes of a psychopath who is stalking her chichi coterie.

The convoluted plot of *Eyes* begins after a two-plus–minutes intro during which the stylized eyes logo stares at the audience while Barbra Streisand is heard

In his leisure detective outfit

singing the film's theme song, "Prisoner." Streisand was to have played the lead, at the behest of her boyfriend *du jour*, Jon Peters, the producer of the film (his second after *A Star Is Born*), but plans changed, and she ended up being heard only as Faye Dunaway became the lead. Dunaway's gaunt look and studied performance, pointed out by virtually every reviewer on the film's release, were on view from scene 1, in which she has black-and-white visions of a woman's murder.

Fade in next to Dunaway, as Laura Mars, at her latest exhibition at a SoHo gallery in Manhattan, with Tommy Lee Jones sidling up to her and introducing himself as a police detective doing an investigation, not long after her manager, Donald Phelps (René Auberjonois), tells her of the killing of her editor. Jones's enigmatic character, John Neville, is partial to turtlenecks and three-piece Armani suits and appears to be quite at home discussing art and mingling with the beautiful people. He breaks the ice in *Eyes* with the following bit of chitchat (he may or may not know that it is the photographer herself he is addressing, but his crafty demeanor and body language

Jones and Dunaway appear moments away from danger.

They meet again at one of Laura's photo shoots, with each knowing more than is being revealed.

Soon she's asking for his protection from a stalker . . .

. . . and he commits a cardinal police sin: giving her his gun.

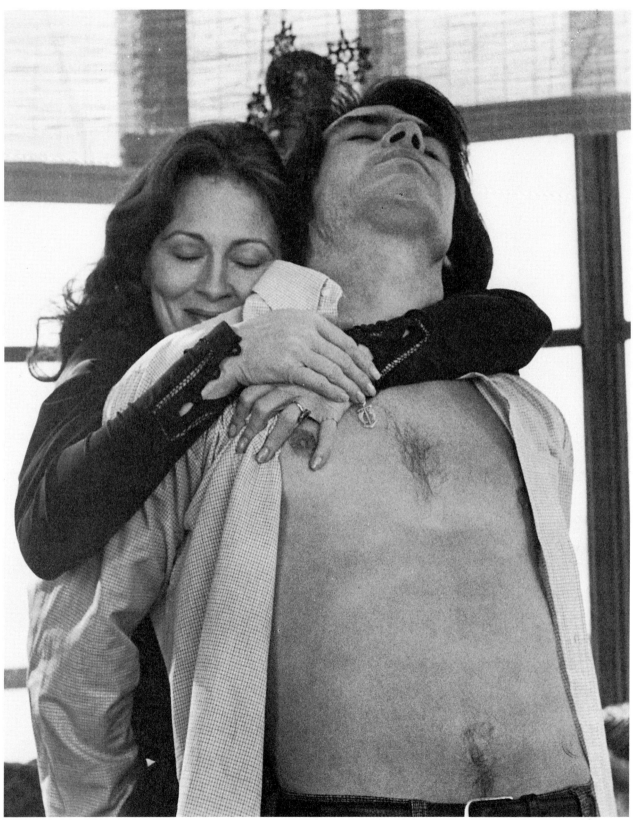

Laura shows her deep appreciation for his help against the unknown assailant before "seeing" the truth.

seem to indicate he does): "I think it's really tragic this is the kind of stuff passing for art these days. High passel rip-off." She: "Are you a critic?" He: "No. Do you know the artist? I'd really be interested in finding out what kind of frustrated voyeur she really is."

Laura later has visions of yet another killing—of a woman who turns out to be her friend and associate but, unbeknownst to Laura, was having an affair with the latter's grasping ex-husband, Michael Reisler. (Reisler was played by Raul Julia, who, for whatever reason, decided to pretentiously have himself billed solely as "R.J." in the opening credits and in the advertising.) Rushing to her friend's apartment, Laura finds her murdered—stabbed through the eye. Neville puts in another appearance, and she relates her hysterical claim of having "seen" the killing. When she asks whether she's under arrest, he responds nonchalantly, "I didn't even frisk you yet." Later, after Laura is menaced by her brooding ex-husband, who has demanded money and has become hostile, Neville becomes increasingly protective of her—and even gives her his service revolver for security! (That certainly appears to be against any known police regulation.) Polite to the extreme, Neville begins dating Laura. "It's completely unprofessional of me to be walking in the woods with you," he tells her. "I'm supposed to be catching a killer."

The two become lovers, but not before two of her models are stabbed to death and Phelps meets a similar fate. Laura has "seen" each murder through the killer's eyes. Suspicion then shifts to Tommy Ludlow (Brad Dourif), Laura's bedraggled and shifty-eyed chauffeur,

who happens to be an ex-con and somewhat unstable, but he soon dies in a police chase. Neville then reassures Laura that the danger is over, although in a psychic flash she later "sees" the killer approaching her apartment. When Neville makes an appearance, it soon becomes evident that he has become unhinged and is a schizo who recalls his father killing his mother when he was a child. The psychopathic half of Neville hates Laura for exploiting death in her photo, while the rational half insists, "I'm the one you want," and that she shoot him—with the service revolver he left with her. Done and done, and the closing credits roll as La Streisand wails her title hit once again.

This was to be the first of a number of starring roles for Jones which found him giving strong support to assorted leading ladies—when he's not doing his trademark movie psychos with various agendas. *Variety* called him "an inspired bit of casting," while Janet Maslin, in the *New York Times*, noted: "High-minded artistic fluttering . . . comes so naturally to [Faye] Dunaway that Tommy Lee Jones, as a down-to-earth, soothing cop, is not just a good foil but an indispensable one. Without his stabilizing presence, the movie might well have turned into a *Network* set in the netherworld." In *Time*, critic Frank Rich wrote: "The acting is out of a '50s B movie. In the effort to create as many suspects as possible, [Irvin] Kershner has directed most of his cast to come on as twitchy psychopaths. . . . As the film's only ostensibly solid citizen, Jones shows at least some restraint. Then again, anyone would look calm playing opposite Dunaway."

Ad for the film as it was about to go into production (note that it is called simply *"Eyes"*) and one for the released movie, in which both stars get billed twice!

60

FAYE DUNAWAY
TOMMY LEE JONES

A GREAT MYSTERY SUSPENSE THRILLER!

EYES
OF LAURA MARS

COLUMBIA PICTURES PRESENTS A JON PETERS PRODUCTION · AN IRVIN KERSHNER FILM
FAYE DUNAWAY
TOMMY LEE JONES
"EYES OF LAURA MARS"
with BRAD DOURIF · RENE AUBERJONOIS · R.J.
Screenplay by JOHN CARPENTER and DAVID ZELAG GOODMAN · Story by JOHN CARPENTER
Executive Producer JACK H. HARRIS · Associate Producer LAURA ZISKIN · Directed by IRVIN KERSHNER
Love Theme from "Eyes of Laura Mars" (Prisoner) Sung by BARBRA STREISAND · Music by ARTIE KANE
Produced by JON PETERS

Soundtrack available on Columbia Records and Tapes   Read the Bantam Book
This film may be too intense for younger audiences.   © 1978 COLUMBIA PICTURES INDUSTRIES, INC.

Columbia
Pictures

No one admitted once the film begins.

COAL MINER'S DAUGHTER (1980): As "teenage" Mooney Lynn with Sissy Spacek as his child bride, Loretta

8

COAL MINER'S DAUGHTER

UNIVERSAL PICTURES, 1980

CAST

Sissy Spacek (*Loretta Lynn*), Tommy Lee Jones (*Doolittle Lynn*), Beverly D'Angelo (*Patsy Cline*), Levon Helm (*Ted Webb*), Phyllis Boyens (*Clara Webb*), Bill Anderson Jr., Foister Dickerson, Malla McCown, Pamela McCown and Kevin Salvilla (*Webb children*), William Sanderson (*Lee Dollarhide*), Sissy Lucas, Pat Patterson, Brian Warf, Elizabeth Wilson (*Loretta's children*), Robert Elkins (*Bobby Day*), Bob Hannah (*Charlie Dick*), Ernest Tubb (*Himself*), Jennifer Beasley (*Patsy Lynn*), Jessica Beasley (*Peggy Lynn*), Merle Kilgore (*Cowboy at Tootsie's*), Susan Kingsley (*Girl at fairground*), Michael Baish (*Storekeeper*), David Gray (*Doc Turner*), Royce Clark (*Hugh Cherry*), Dave Thornhill, Don Ballinger, Zeke Dawson, Gene Dunlap, Durwood Edwards, Chuck Flynn, Lonnie Godfrey, and Bob Hempker (*Coal Miner's Band*), Danny Faircloth, Charles Gore, Doug Mauseman, Mike Noble, Daniel Sarenana, and Billy West (*Patsy Cline Band*), and Gary Parker, Billy Strange, Bruce Newman, Grant Turner, Frank Mitchell, Jackie Lynn Wright, Rhonda Rhoton, Vernon Oxford, Ron Hensley, Doug Bledsoe, Aubrey Wells, Russell Varner, Tommie O'Donnell, Lou Headley, Ruby Caudrill, Charles Kahlenberg, Alice McGeachy, Ken Riley, Jim Webb.

CREDITS

Executive producer, Bob Larson; *producer*, Bernard Schwartz; *associate producer*, Zelda Barron; *director*,

Mooney Lynn promises stardom for talented young wife Loretta

Michael Apted; *screenplay,* Tom Rickman; *based on the autobiography by* Loretta Lynn with George Vecsey; *cinematographer,* Ralf D. Bode; *production designer,* John W. Corso; *music supervisor,* Owen Bradley; *songs performed by* Sissy Spacek, Beverly D'Angelo, Levon Helm, Kitty Wells, Red Foley; *editor,* Arthur Schmidt. Technicolor; *running time,* 124 minutes.

Among the handful of really fine movie biographies, *Coal Miner's Daughter* boasted an Oscar-winning performance by Sissy Spacek as rags-to-riches country-music great Loretta Lynn, from shy teenager to her powerhouse forties, and a portrayal matched in quality by Tommy Lee Jones. As her impetuous down-home boyfriend, called Mooney—as in "Moonshine," Jones woos her, marries her, adores her, gives her the confidence to blossom, becomes her manager, and is credited with making her a star.

Nineteen-year-old backwoods romeo Doolittle (Mooney) Lynn has returned to Butcher Hollow, Kentucky, from World War II. He sets about charming thirteen-year-old Loretta Webb, the apple of her coalminer father's eye (he's played by Levon Helm, of the rock group The Band), and gets her dirt-poor parents'

somewhat reluctant approval to marry her. The wedding night is a rocky one, but Mooney is gentle with his young bride. Eventually, she goes off with him to Washington State to work in a logging camp. He's determined not to get trapped into mining again. He has three choices that have become local Appalachian legend: "Coal mine, moonshine, or movin' on down the line." He tells her as he leaves, "Ain't nothin' for me 'cept a chestful of coal dust. I'll be an old man time I'm forty."

Jump to six years and four children later. They're back

Appalachian family photo: Tommy Lee Jones and Sissy Spacek with parents Phyllis Boyens and Levon Helm and the siblings

in Kentucky, where Loretta has developed into a good housewife, and Mooney (Loretta calls him Doo throughout), taken by the songs she sings around the place, tricks her into appearing with a local band at a roadhouse. Enjoying the limelight, she lets him persuade her to cut a record of "Honky Tonk Girl," a song she wrote. Mooney mails the record to local radio stations and follows up with unannounced drop-ins with country-music deejays, who find themselves tickled by the shyly talkative Loretta. "Honky Tonk Girl" becomes a hit, and

As Mooney, brooding as his wife's career hits the stratosphere

Mooney steers her to Nashville and the *Grand Ole Opry,* where she is befriended by her idol, Patsy Cline (a stellar performance by Beverly D'Angelo). As Loretta's career blooms and she acquires an entourage and bigger and bigger buses for her tours, Mooney, determined not to become "Mr. Loretta Lynn," begins drinking and carousing but never loses his adoration of his wife. Shattered when learning that chum Patsy Cline has been killed in a plane crash, Loretta finds that despite Mooney's warnings, her own driving ambition is dogged increasingly by pills and barbiturates. "Gettin' there is one thing; bein' there is another," Mooney tells her in a confrontation outside her tour bus at one of the stops. "My job is done, baby. I'll just get another." "I'll quit!" the now-driven star responds. "Successful people don't quit, baby," he replies.

Eventually, Loretta collapses onstage. Mooney hovers over her during her breakdown and ultimate recovery (passed over rather quickly in the film), leading to the renewal of their relationship, and she ultimately returns to the stage with her autobiographical song, the title of her book and of this uplifting movie, directed by Britisher Michael Apted. Sissy Spacek, as has become well known, did all of her own singing—and there was lots of it—in the Loretta Lynn mold, and this, along with the performances, impressed the majority of reviewers. Aside from the star's Oscar, there were six other nominations, for Best Picture (*Ordinary People* won that year), screenplay adaptation, cinematography, editing, art direction/set decoration, and sound.

The British publication *Monthly Film Bulletin* said: "Unexpected is the way in which the central relationship, superbly played by Sissy Spacek and Tommy Lee Jones, respects both characters by refusing to tailor them to romantic (or even feminist) conventions." Kathleen Carroll (New York *Daily News*) observed: "As young Doolittle, Tommy Lee Jones is so charged up that it's easy to imagine him sweeping any woman off her feet, certainly a gawky thirteen-year-old girl. . . . [Later] Jones brings a special warmth and a rugged charm to the character of Doolittle, who balks at being just one of his wife's hangers-on and tries to rule the roost while giving her the love and encouragement she needs to deal with the demands of fame."

In *Newsweek*, David Ansen opined: "Jones, who looks like a hillbilly Nureyev, gives a strong, subtle performance, finally making good on the promise he showed several years back in *Jackson County Jail*." And critic Rex Reed, finding that "it's a genuine pleasure to see a film as spirited, honest and life-affirming," gushed over Sissy Spacek. "She is matched every step of the way by Tommy Lee Jones, who goes from ambitious 'good ol' boy' to lonely, middle-aged backstage husband as he creates Loretta's stardom, then tries to exist like a man in the shadows behind her pin spots."

Jones and Spacek would work together again in the mid nineties in his first film as a director, *The Good Old Boys*.

Mooney overseeing one of Loretta's sessions with Ernest Tubb (playing himself) and fellow musicians

9

BACK ROADS

CBS THEATRICAL FILMS, 1981

CAST

Sally Field (*Amy Post*), Tommy Lee Jones (*Elmor Pratt*), David Keith (*Mason*), Miriam Colón (*Angel*), Michael Gazzo (*Tazio*), Dan Shor (*Spivey*), M. Emmet Walsh (*Arthur*), Barbara Babcock (*Ricky's mom*), Nell Carter (*Waitress*), Alex Colón (*Enrique*), Lee de Broux (*Red*), Ralph Seymour (*Gosler*), Royce Applegate (*Father*), Bruce M. Fischer (*Ezra*), John Dennis Johnston (*Gilly*), Don "Red" Barry (*Pete*), Billy Jacoby (*Boy thief*), Eric Laneuville (*Pinball Wizard*), Brian Frishman (*Bleitz*), Diane Sommerfield (*Liz*), Henry Slate (*Grover*), Matthew Campion (*Stromberg*), Tony Ganios (*Bartini*), Lee McLaughlin (*Deputy*), Arthur Pugh (*Taper*), Gerry Okuneff (*Oren*), Louie Nicholas (*Burt*), Cherie Brantley (*Ellen*), Jim Bailey (*Billy*), and Fred Baldwin, Billy Holliday, Barbara Thompson, Buddy Thompson, Phil Gordon, Mike Barton, Richard Charles Boyle, Sherrie Whitman, Lupita Cornego, Bob E. Hannah, David Powledge, Eliott Keener, David Pellette, David Dahlgren, John Jackson, John Wilmot, Jack Shadix, Leonardo J. Noriega, Joe Ford, Woody Watson, Duke Alexander.

CREDITS

Meta-Films Associates in association with Marion Rosenberg. *Producer*, Ronald Shedlo; *director*, Martin Ritt; *screenplay*, Gary Devore; *cinematographer*, John A. Alonzo; *production designer*, Walter Scott Herndon; *music*, Henry Mancini; *song "Ask Me No Questions (I'll Tell You No Lies)"* *by* Mancini and Marilyn and Alan Bergman, *performed by* Sue Rainey; *editor*, Sidney Levin. DeLuxe color; *running time*, 95 minutes.

"I am what I am," Tommy Lee Jones, as shiftless, glass-jawed, ex-boxer Elmor Pratt, tells Sally Field, as feisty, spike-heeled, heart-of-gold hooker Amy Post, in this road movie that kicks off at a garish honky-tonk bar in Mobile, Alabama, "and I got news for you, sweetheart. So are you." She has just picked up Pratt, a drunken john, in hopes of turning a dishonest buck and has angrily thrown him out after finding that he's broke. Anxious to make amends, he decks one of her prospective clients, only to learn he is a plainclothes cop. Thus they begin an uneasy alliance. Warned to stay away from her small son by the woman who adopted him, Amy strikes out for California, hoping to become a manicurist. Elmor, having lost his job, tags along on the rambunctious odyssey. "We're gonna be travelin' on wit and grit, gal, and I sure as hell hope and pray to the good Lord in heaven you ain't left yours back in Mobile."

Their hitchhiking, bickering, and brawling finds them running out on lunch checks, hustling bus money, hopping freight trains, rolling drunks, washing dishes, selling blood, and admiring each other something fierce—if not overtly falling in love. Along the back roads, Elmor lets a bit of his life come to light. Amy learns that he had been married once. "Her name was Dixie," he reveals. "Met her on a Tuesday, married her on a Wednesday. Didn't want me to get away." Soon, as in true *It Happened One*

As Elmor Pratt, ex-boxer with a glass jaw

Elmor Pratt and Amy Post at loose ends on the road . . .

. . . and mixing somewhat soggy fun and games.

Night fashion, while hitching somewhat unsuccessfully, Amy hikes her skirt, and they are given a lift by a good-hearted but naive sailor (David Keith), with whom she begins flirting to rile Elmor. But as she and the sailor visit a fairground in a nearby town, it falls to Elmor to save her from being raped by four of the sailor's buddies. When they land in Brownsville, Texas, Amy leaves Elmor and tries turning tricks for spending money until she is warned off by a local madam. (Elmor earlier had called Amy nothing more than a whore, to which she shot back: "A whore is a sixteen-year-old girl with a bad reputation. I am a hustler!")

Elmor meanwhile manages to set up a fight through a local promoter but is relieved of his winnings by a bunch of punks sent by the madam when Amy persists in working her territory. And so it is back to rolling drunks. "I don't wanna be around you if you keep robbin' people," she tells him. "We ain't Bonnie and Clyde." In despair, Amy talks about returning to Mobile and her son, who most likely doesn't even know her, annoying Elmor, who, in a local bar, proceeds to auction her off jokingly to local rednecks, then rescue her when he realizes he's in love. And the two hit the road once more, thumbing a ride to El Dorado.

Warily back to the ring in a tank town when the dough runs out

In *Newsweek*, critic David Ansen found that "[Martin] Ritt adroitly meshes his idealized protagonists with down-home backdrops of bars and brothels and seedy bus stations. With the spunky Field at her most engaging and Jones exuding ruffian sexual charisma, the chemistry seems perfect for a gracefully funky romantic frolic. *Back Roads* only partly fulfills the promise." And in the New York *Daily News*, Kathleen Carroll wrote: "Fields is adorably sassy even if her character makes no sense. Jones is even more engaging with his easy-going backwoods charm perhaps because he, at least, looks the part. But this is one road movie that goes strictly nowhere."

Back Roads, "anchored only by the abrasive presence of Tommy Lee Jones," wrote critic Tom Milne of Britain's *Monthly Film Bulletin*, was the maiden venture of CBS Theatrical Films, one of several abortive ones on which the network had embarked at various times. But despite a number of important notices, like Vincent Canby's *New York Times* review, calling the film "extremely appealing and occasionally gutsy and very funny . . . probably one of the most stylish comedies you'll ever see about the joys of third-ratedness," the Martin Ritt movie proved not promising enough for CBS to make a go of it in filmmaking.

Shot primarily in Mobile, Alabama, and Brownsville, Texas, *Back Roads* was the movie on the set of which Jones met his photojournalist wife, Kimberlea, who had landed a tiny part in the Brownsville filming.

Elmor and Amy plan the bus trip to Brownsville.

10

SAVAGE ISLANDS

U.S. title: NATE AND HAYES

PARAMOUNT PICTURES, 1983

CAST

Tommy Lee Jones (*Capt. "Bully" Hayes*), Michael O'Keefe (*Nathaniel Williamson*), Max Phipps (*Ben Pease*), Jenny Seagrove (*Sophie*), Grant Tilly (*Count von Rittenberg*), Peter Rowley (*Louis Beck*), Bill Johnson (*Reverend Williamson*), Kate Harcourt (*Mrs. Williamson*), Reg Ruka (*Moaka*), Roy Billing (*Auctioneer*), Bruce Allpress (*Mr. Blake*), David Letch (*Ratbag*), Prince Tui Teka (*King Owatopi*), Pudji Waseso (*Fong*), Peter Vere Jones (*Gunboat captain*), Tom Vanderlass (*Count's lieutenant*), and Mark Hadlow, Philip Gordon, Norman Fairley, Warwick Simmons, Paul Farrell, Frank Taurua, Norman Keesing, Robert Bruce, Timothy Lee, Peter Bell, Peter Diamond, John Rush, Grant Price, Karl Bradley.

CREDITS

Phillips Whitehouse Productions. *Producers,* Lloyd Phillips and Rob Whitehouse; *director,* Ferdinand Fairfax; *screenplay,* John Hughes and David Odell, *based on a story by* Lloyd Phillips; *cinematographer,* Tony Imi; *production designer,* Maurice Cain; *music,* Trevor Jones, *performed by* the London Symphony Orchestra, *conducted by* Marcus Dods; *editor,* John Shirley. In color; *running time,* 99 minutes.

In this lighthearted, buoyant swashbuckler, filmed in New Zealand and Fiji, Tommy Lee Jones has a good old time as an infamous nineteenth-century brigand, Capt. William Hayes ("Bully—call me Bully"), who trades guns to South Pacific natives hostile to the Spanish Empire. He strides through the role with panache and more than a touch of irreverence, beginning the tale by blithely wiping out practically an entire female-dominated tribe after a gun sale goes bad. Escaping, he falls into the scummy hands of blackguard Ben Pease, a fellow bootlegger and slave trader (played by Max Phipps) who once was his partner but now is working as an agent for Spain, and is condemned to death. To a prison journalist, roguish

Hayes recounts his story: "Are you saying I'm a pirate? Good—cause I am, and a damn good one, too. Though I never flew the skull and crossbones—that's for your fictioneers. I have sought pleasure and profit all of my life at sea, with no desire for any man's law."

A lengthy flashback follows, taking the viewer back eighteen months, when Hayes was engaged to transport a young couple, Sophie, a spunky English girl, and Nathaniel, a stodgy American missionary, to their wedding on a remote island run by missionaries. (It is somewhat disconcerting to see at least one of the half-dressed "savages" there wearing spectacles, but that's just one of the freewheeling touches.) Hayes's rival, Pease, on a

Bully and his men prepare for a spot of plundering on a native island.

slave raid, interrupts the ceremony, and the reverend, who happens to be the groom's uncle, and all the guests are shot. Nathaniel is left for dead by Pease, who abducts Sophie. Though wounded, Nathaniel makes his way back to Hayes's ship and, after first blaming him for the massacre, vows vengeance against Hayes's old enemy. Nate and Hayes eventually catch up with Pease in Samoa, where he has been arranging a meeting between Count von Rittenberg, a German naval commander, and the obese native king whose island the count wants for a safe harbor. After Bully turns up with his crew and Nate in time to save Sophie from a sacrifice to the king as Pease and the count hightail it to the latter's ironclad gunboat, he and the boys sail off in nasty Pease's own boat. The battle is soon joined: the old salt, the young landlubber, and the damsel in distress (she's suddenly shed her virginal white wedding gown for a shirt, jeans, and suspenders) on the trail of the odious villain on the high seas. In a spirited battle with cannons ablaze, Nate and Hayes manage to elude the German gunboat but sneak back and board the vessel for a dandy hand-to-hand encounter with muskets, pistols, sabers, and even a Ninja-type swordsman (one of Bully's crew). The whole escapade ends with Bully booby-trapping the ironclad and, after escaping back to Pease's stolen four-master, watching with Nate, Sophie, and the crew as it blows up. As he finishes his tale to his biographer, guards come to take him to the gallows. His hanging, though, is thwarted at the end as Nate and Sophie, disguised as a clergyman and a gun-toting nun, come to his rescue so that further adventures can be sought.

Bearded, jocular Tommy Lee Jones yo-ho-hos it (with

O'Keefe and Jones in the title roles

Tommy Lee Jones (as Hayes) makes his escape with Jenny Seagrove (as the once demure Sophie in virginal white) and swashbuckling greenhorn Nathaniel Williamson (Michael O'Keefe) following massacre.

On shipboard, Bully Hayes makes a play for receptive Sophie to Nate's annoyance.

a sometimes sinister chuckle) as a dashing Burt Lancaster or Errol Flynn wannabe in this energetic attempt to breathe new life into filmdom's once-popular Saturday matinee pirate flicks, which hadn't had much contemporary luck since Robert Shaw's box-office flop *Swashbuckler* in 1976 (or Roman Polanski's equally disastrous *Pirates*, starring Walter Matthau, a decade later). Shown in the United States, ever so briefly, as *Nate and Hayes*, Jones's 1983 epic—hoping to find the audience enjoyed by *Raiders of the Lost Ark*—sank from sight and has seldom been seen since. It is, however, available on home video.

Many reviewers were amused by the plot twists and by the star. *The Hollywood Reporter* felt that "most central to the film's success is Tommy Lee Jones. His physical prowess has never been in doubt, but rarely, if ever, has he been allowed to exhibit his rambunctious sense of humor onscreen before, and he has a field day with his role." Historian (and pirate movie buff) William K. Everson wrote in *Films in Review:* "It starts out in a seemingly savage manner, and it perhaps takes a little too long to establish that it is really all tongue-in-cheek. But once under way, it's a delight. There is violence aplenty,

Sailing for the final confrontation with his freebooting nemesis, with the dubious Nate and the confident Sophie (having slipped out of her wedding gown for something more appropriate for the occasion, although where she found the outfit remains a mystery)

Bully does some serious parrying with German naval commander Count von Rittenberg (Grant Tilly).

but most of it is either exaggerated or implied—though so skillfully done that many will feel they've seen more bloodletting than they have. . . . The color photography of Fiji and New Zealand is stunning, and the performance of Tommy Lee Jones both athletic and winning."

Other critics were less complimentary. Vincent Canby (*New York Times*) observed: "Though Mr. Jones, Mr. O'Keefe, and Jenny Seagrove, who plays a spunky young woman named Sophie (which allows for a joke about a choice she must make), are attractive, lively actors, the movie is no fun at all. An old man with a peg leg would have no trouble keeping ahead of the plot, which, among other things, involves cannibals, sailing ships, one early ironclad warship, and a sequence in which Hayes trades guns for gold with Polynesians whom he describes as 'anticolonialists.' As pirates go, Hayes, it seems, is a bit left of center." Kevin Thomas (*Los Angeles Times*) thought that "[it] could easily have been terrific. . . . But *Nate and Hayes* drowns in excessive violence and Trevor Jones' loud, bombastic score."

11

THE RIVER RAT

PARAMOUNT PICTURES, 1984

CAST

Tommy Lee Jones (*Billy McCain*), Brian Dennehy (*Doc Cole*), Martha Plimpton (*Jonsy*), Shawn Smith (*Wexel*), Nancy Lee Owen (*Vadie*), Norman Bennett (*Sheriff Cal*), Tony Frank (*Poley*), Angela Bolling (*Joyce*), Roger Copeland (*Young Billy*), Tommy Burlison (*Whitey*), Tamara Hartley (*Young Joyce*), Louise Anderson (*Wexel's aunt*), Melissa Hart (*Peggy*), Mary Harper (*Old woman*), Michael Shepard (*Cajun Sheriff*), Pete Renaday (*Cajun doctor*), Louis R. Plante and Rod Britt (*Cajun deputies*), and Robert Le Blanc, Craig Cruse, Bill O'Neal, Creston B. Parker, Melissa Davis, Kenyatta Beasley, Charles C. Beasley.

CREDITS

Larson/Rickman production in association with the Sundance Institute. *Executive producer,* Michael Apted; *producer,* Bob Larson; *writer-director,* Tom Rickman; *cinematographer:* Jan Kiesser; *production designer:* John J. Lloyd; *music,* Mike Post; *song "The River's Song" by* Post and Stephen Geyer, *performed by* Joey Scarbury; *editor:* Steve Mirkovich. Technicolor; *running time,* 93 minutes.

The setting is along the Kentucky backwaters of the Mississippi. The title refers to a wreck of a boat that Tommy Lee Jones, as sullen parolee Billy McCain, is restoring with Jonsy (Martha Plimpton in her film debut), his tomboy daughter whom he hadn't met during the thirteen years he spent in prison for an accidental killing. Billy, guarded, is trying to pick up the pieces of his life and is struggling to establish a rapport with self-reliant Jonsy, who has been living with her grandmother, who runs a riverside tackle shop. Jonsy's mother, Joyce, long gone, was a teenager when young Billy got her pregnant. Slowly Billy opens up to Jonsy about his earlier life, his buddy Whitey, and Joyce, who had been running around with them. "It was Whitey, Joyce, and me . . . foolin' around like we always do. Had us a picnic. Whitey stole some beer someplace. There's a ole widow woman lived on the river. Us kids grew up havin' nightmares 'bout her. Husband died. Left her millions of dollars." It soon comes out that while the three had broken into the old woman's house to steal the money, she was killed, and Billy and Whitey took off in her car with the loot. The car ran a police roadblock in Louisiana and crashed at the entrance of a Cajun cemetery. Billy was thrown clear, but Whitey died. Billy scooped up the money as the car burst into flames and, with the police in hot pursuit, ran into the cemetery and stuffed it into a coffin with a body about to be buried.

Doc Cole, a crooked prison doctor, ultimately arranges for Billy to get paroled, feeling that the latter would lead him to the stolen money that Billy said was burned up years before with Whitey. Doc turns up at Billy's place, and the two clash over the money in a skiff on the river (an imaginatively filmed confrontation from

THE RIVER RAT (1984): On the set with young newcomer Martha Plimpton

As withdrawn parolee Billy McCain, having little luck establishing a rapport with Jonsy, the twelve-year-old daughter he's yet to get to know . . .

afar so that their words are just a faint murmur). Doc falls overboard, and Billy leaves him for dead.

Billy, meanwhile, has become not only a pal to Jonsy but also the father she never knew and with another of her chums, Wexel, a black youngster from nearby, prepares for an adventure on the *River Rat* to Memphis. Before they take off downriver, Wexel comes upon Doc, dragging himself ashore, but keeps the news to himself. Poley Bass, a local redneck who never cottoned to Billy and his family, takes Doc in and wheedles information about the stolen money out of him. Doc beats him to death and plants evidence on the body incriminating Billy, then takes off in pursuit. Memphis is where Joyce is now living, and Billy pays her a visit to try to clear the air after all these years and to reintroduce her to Jonsy; he finds her unresponsive. Billy and Jonsy, with Wexel, who has rejoined them after failing to contact relatives in town, soon find Doc threatening them, and at gunpoint he forces himself into their adventure on the *River Rat* as they make their way to Cajun country and the old cemetery and grave where Billy hid the money before being captured. "Man's crazy, baby," Billy confides in Jonsy. "He's a killer." Camping out overnight, the group finds itself in the path of a runaway barge that explodes. Doc

doesn't make it back aboard Billy's boat, which heads toward Louisiana, where, at an outdoor riverside celebration, Billy and Jonsy are taken in by the music. "You got dancin' in prison?" she asks him. "We got everything in prison," he replies.

Ultimately, they make their way to the Cajun cemetery and locate the overgrown grave. As Billy frantically endeavors to dig up the money he'd stashed there years before, Jonsy pleads with him to begin a new life with her. "I ain't meant to have a life. All I can do is run," he tells her.

Suddenly, the seemingly indestructible Doc turns up, badly wounds Billy, and grabs the uncovered loot. Then he goes after a terrified Jonsy and Wexel but is knocked down by Billy. As the police show up, Doc, with a severe, life-threatening case of poison ivy from his earlier run-in with Poley, makes his painful way into the rushes, and Billy ends up in the local jail, where he is patched up. Ultimately, Doc is captured with the money in hand, Billy is exonerated from charges of killing Poley, and he, Jonsy, and Wexel head for home on the *River Rat*.

This rural idyll involving initially a father-daughter relationship and later turning into a suspense–murder thriller was found by *Variety* to be "a worthwhile entry in

. . . but doing some fix-up work on their broken-down *River Rat* provides a conversational opening.

Writer and first-time director Tom Rickman (who wrote the screenplay to *Coal Miner's Daughter*) discusses a scene with Martha and Tommy Lee.

Billy prepares for the trip downriver with tomboy Jonsy and her playmate Wexel (Shawn Smith) . . .

the swelling field of rural dramas. . . . Tommy Lee Jones makes Billy a likable, sympathetic and moving character." Especially charming was an interlude during the travels when Jonsy decides to go skinny-dipping in the Mississippi and Billy happens upon her as she is flirting with a crew member of a passing barge. Jonsy, covering herself while standing waist-deep in the water, sasses him: "Guess you're worried about incest, huh? It's just natural to be worried about it, I mean." "You don't even know what those words mean," Billy shouts to her from shore. She responds: "You wouldn't believe how many families got incest. If it bothers you, the best thing is to come right out in the open and talk about it." Billy tells her: "There are some things that you're not supposed to be talkin' about. You don't talk about things like that just like there's somethin' else." And she counters: "Maybe if you had you wouldn'ta gotten Joyce in trouble."

The River Rat was not widely shown theatrically. Following its opening in San Francisco, *Chronicle* reviewer Judy Stone wrote: "there was enough going just

. . . but soon find that Billy's nemesis (Brian Dennehy) has caught up with them and insists on keeping them all close by.

with the story of Jonsy and her long-absent father . . . without a murderous and far-fetched treasure hunt being dragged in for what someone must have thought was box-office appeal." Critic Stone continued: "Tommy Lee Jones as the reserved and withdrawn Billy and Martha Plimpton, whose unconventional pertness is a welcome change from conventional teenage cuties, establish an interesting rapport that should have been developed more fully."

First-time director Tom Rickman, who also wrote this tale laced with Gothic trappings, pervasive evil, coming-of-age, and redemption, was best known up to this time as the Oscar-nominated screenwriter for Tommy Lee Jones's earlier *Coal Miner's Daughter*.

Docking in Memphis, Jonsy and Billy are questioned by the local law (Norman Bennett).

12

BLACK MOON RISING

NEW WORLD PICTURES, 1986

CAST

Tommy Lee Jones (*Quint*), Linda Hamilton (*Nina*), Robert Vaughn (*Edward Ryland*), Richard Jaeckel (*Earl Windom*), Lee Ving (*Marvin Ringer*), Bubba Smith (*Johnson*), Dan Shor (*Billy Lyons*), William Sanderson (*Tyke Thayden*), Keenan Wynn (*Iron John*), Nick Cassavetes (*Luis*), Richard Angarola (*Dr. Melato*), Don Opper (*Frenchie*), William Marquez (*Reynoso*), David Pressman (*Kid at grocery store*), Stanley De Santiis (*The mover*), Edward Parone (*Mr. Emilio*), and Al White, Bill Moody, Townsend Coleman, Dalton Cathey, Frank Dent, Steve Fifield, Dave Adams, Lana Lancaster, E. J. Castillo, Peterson Banks, Rudy Daniels, Carl Ciarfalio, Don Pulford, Vincent Pandoliano, Lisa London, David Donham, Doug MacHugh, Eric Trules.

CREDITS

Producers, Joel B. Michaels and Douglas Curtis; *director*, Harley Cokliss; *screenplay*, John Carpenter, Desmond Nakano, and William Gray, *from a story by* Carpenter; *cinematographer*, Mischa Suslov; *visual effects photography*, Jonathan Seay; *production designer*, Bryan Ryman; *music*, Lalo Schifrin; *song "Sleeping With the Enemy" by* Chari Brandon and Jack Littlejohn, *performed by* Brandon; *editor*, Todd Ramsay. CFI color; *running time*, 99 minutes.

BLACK MOON RISING (1986): As Sam Quint, dallying briefly with Linda Hamilton, as comely Nina, master car thief

In this engaging but rather hole-filled caper movie cowritten by John Carpenter with Tommy Lee Jones as a high-tech thief and a snazzy prototype of a jet car, the Black Moon, as its chief assets, logic and credibility become dispensable—especially with a climactic chase in the car from the basement of a skyscraper to the top! Jones, trying his hand at Bruce Willis–type action hero, plays good ol' boy Quint, sort of an unofficial thief for the feds. Quint has ripped off some incriminating data tapes from the mob in Vegas, and while running from vicious Marvin Ringer (Lee Ving) and a small army of killers, he stashes the stuff in a sleek, candy-bar-shaped sports car, a prototype fueled by water. It is being taken to Hollywood by its designer, Earl Windom, but is presently stolen by Nina, an enigmatic car thief working for a crooked, three-piece-suit industrialist named Ryland.

Pressured by his "employers" to retrieve their vital evidence in seventy-two hours or else, Quint, with Windom in tow, goes in hot pursuit of Nina and the Moon, and when he catches up with her, he and she find they're made for one another and they fall into bed, unaware that Ryland has had her place bugged and is videotaping the entire thing. The morning after their night together,

Keenan Wynn, in one of his last roles, shares with Tommy Lee some tricks of the trade in trying to crack the sophisticated car-theft operation.

Quint reminds her, "We have a lot in common, you know; we're both thieves." She asks him, "And what do you steal?" He replies, "This and that. Actually, as soon as my current obligations are taken care of, I'm retiring." She: "And what do retired thieves do?" He: "They get away." Now there's the matter of her murderous boss and his goons, who want the Moon and will stop at nothing to get it. Ryland, after all, owns a pair of immense towers in downtown L.A. which he uses as a high-rise auto-parts chop shop and where he garages his very expensive stolen cars.

A gussied-up road movie, the whole enterprise ends in a predictable shoot-out following a commando-like raid (Quint has hooked up with the car's designer, played by Richard Jaeckel, and his associate) and a not-so-predictable leap, with Quint and Nina driving the Moon from the sixtieth floor of one tower to the other. How the mob boys who have been chasing Quint happen to be waiting in an abandoned skyscraper exactly where the Moon would land is never explained, but it sets the scene for the climactic brawl between Quint and the indefatigable Ringer.

This modern-day swashbuckler, following his earlier *Nate and Hayes,* allowed freelance thief Jones (looking less assured, as his character was written, than in most of his roles) to have a great old time with clever banter, whether fleeing a hail of bullets in the opening scenes or "flying" the Moon in the closing ones, squealing Moon's wheels, putting the make on his pouty costar, getting beaten to a pulp (twice) by one set of bad guys or the other, or crossing verbal swords with the malevolent villain Vaughn. Action director Harley Cokliss, meanwhile, puts his formula yarn through its paces efficiently. The film also marked one of the last roles for veteran actor Keenan Wynn, in an extraneous, single-scene role as a dying old codger who apparently once was a colleague of Quint's and gives him some words of advice and clues about the twin towers.

In his review, *New York Times* critic Vincent Canby decided: "Giving the film its class is Mr. Jones, an actor who has been on the brink of real star status for too many years. . . . It's time he got his own break. Quint isn't an especially challenging role, but Mr. Jones brings to the performance an easygoing humor and self-assured person-

Jones plans a daring raid to recover the stolen Black Moon, with its designer Richard Jaeckel (*left*) and confederate Don Opper.

ality that are worth probably much more than he was paid. The members of the supporting cast are good, though not in the same league." *The Hollywood Reporter*'s Duane Byrge wrote: "What works best in *Black Moon Rising* is the dialogue, often brisk and funny, and Jones' performance, often deadpan and comic." On the other hand, traditionally grumpy Rex Reed saw it this way: "This movie is so confused that it really isn't about Black Moon at all. It's about Tommy Lee Jones, who only has black moons under his bloodshot eyes. . . . This is a mindless dingbat movie that relies on all the old clichés. . . ."

An amusing sidebar is cowriter John Carpenter's sly homage to trashmeister Harold Robbins, calling a posh restaurant—from where Linda Hamilton is ripping off classy wheels—the Betsy. "Now there was a great car movie!" the New York *Daily News* critic observed in reviewing *Black Moon Rising*.

Surveying his next move in the basement of the skyscraper chop shop

13

THE BIG TOWN

COLUMBIA PICTURES, 1987

CAST

Matt Dillon (*J. C. Cullen*), Diane Lane (*Lorry Dane*), Tommy Lee Jones (*George Cole*), Bruce Dern (*Mr. Edwards*), Lee Grant (*Ferguson Edwards*), Tom Skerritt (*Phil Carpenter*), Suzy Amis (*Aggie Donaldson*), David Marshall Grant (*Sammy Binkley*), Don Francks (*Carl Hooker*), Del Close (*Deacon Daniels*), Meg Hogarth (*Dorothy Cullen*), Cherry Jones (*Ginger McDonald*), Mark Danton (*Prager*), David Elliott (*Cool Guy*), Sean McCann (*Ray McMullin*), Marc Strange (*Madigan*), Don Luke (*Patsy Fuqua*), Sarah Polley (*Christy Donaldson*), and Steve Yorke, Chris Owens, Kevin Fox, Angelo Rizacos, Chris Benson, Gary Farmer, Diego Matamoros, Kirsten Bishop, Ken McGregor, Viki Matthews, Sandy Czapiewski, Marie Siebert, Julie Conte, Alar Adema, Sam Malkin, Robert Morelli, Layne Coleman, Lolita David, Bill Colgate, William Forrest MacDonald, Len Doncheff, Michael Caruana, Richard Comar, Lubomir Mykytiuk, Robert Ramsey Collins, Errol Slue, Gerry Pearson, Hugo Dann, John Evans, J. W. Carroll, Diane Gordon.

CREDITS

A Martin Ransohoff production. *Executive producer,* Gene Craft; *producer,* Martin Ransohoff; *coproducer,* Don Carmody; *director,* Ben Bolt; *screenplay,* Robert Roy Pool; *based on the novel* The Arm *by* Clark Howard; *cinematographer,* Ralf D. Bode; *production designer,* Bill Kenney; *music,* Michael Melvoin; *editor,* Stuart Pappe. In color; *running time,* 110 minutes.

The Big Town, as more than one reviewer pointed out at the time, aimed to be *The Hustler* with dice. It was a small picture that boasted a big-name cast, basically playing lowlifes, which included Tommy Lee Jones, flamboyantly essaying a scowling fifties Chicago gangster; up-and-coming Matt Dillon as a swaggering, Juicy Fruit–chewing hayseed who knew how to make those spotted cubes "talk"; and Diane Lane as a stripteasing tramp who was married to Tommy Lee and making moves on Matt. Lee Grant and Bruce Dern were slumming, too, as a hard-as-nails club owner and her blind

THE BIG TOWN (1987): Tommy Lee Jones running the craps table out of the back room of his Chicago strip joint while Diane Lane as his hard-boiled wife, who headlines the show, looks on and Don Francks prepares to make a bet

husband who bankrolled the freelance crapshooter who blows into town from Nebraska. And the cast also included future "stars" Tom Skerritt (who was to make it to the big time on TV in *Picket Fences* after kicking around for some time) and Cherry Jones (who hit stardom on Broadway several years later in *The Heiress*). A terrific cast in a pedestrian venture by first-time director Ben Bolt.

Adapted from a novel called *The Arm*, it tells the not-overly-original tale of a small-towner with a great arm—for rolling dice. The clean-cut kid called Cully has "the cool," according to his gambling mentor back home, meaning that he just can't seem to lose at craps. So he lights out for Chicago, the Big Town, naïveté and all,

leaving his widowed mom, and falls in with the street-smart Ferguson Edwards and her husband, who own a local joint there and spot a winner when they come across one. Sent to them by his back-home mentor, he's to be their dice-throwing "arm." Cully also gains the eye of strip-joint owner and gambler Cole, enacted with his usual panache and expensive attire by Tommy Lee Jones ("played with his usual scowl," reported Kathleen Carroll in her New York *Daily News* review). But Cole doesn't cotton to being beaten by this young whipper-snapper with hay in his hair.

Cully the Arm has also attracted the girls and quickly finds himself torn between demure single mom Aggie Donaldson and fan-dancing floozy Lorry Dane, who just happens to be gangster Cole's hard-boiled and hard-bodied old lady. Things progress in the underdog-meets-the-sharpies way of all enterprises like this, and ultimately Cully, thanks to Cole's devious, cheating ways, finds himself at the craps table down to his proverbial last dollar. It's manipulative Lorry to the rescue, having freed herself from Cole's grasp. She bankrolls Cully for the big score that brings Cole down. "Your luck is gonna change, son," Cully is warned by the beaten Cole with hate in his eyes. "Bet on it!"

There's also a convoluted subplot here involving a shady gambler named Phil Carpenter (Tom Skerritt), who years before was responsible for the blinding of Edwards, and a shooting by gangster Cole, who has

thrown in with the Edwardses after losing his joint to Cully's left arm and Lorry's cheating ways, that muddies the film's waters. But, at the wrap-up, Cole is bagged by the cops, Lorry has two-timed still-naive Cully, and Ferguson Edwards has paid off her "arm" with thanks. And it's back to the farm, richer but wiser, for Cully—with Aggie on his arm and big bucks in his jeans.

The Big Town provided a starring showcase for scowling Matt Dillon in his James Dean–early Paul Newman mode, and he's in every scene, along with a relentless soundtrack of rhythm-and-blues favorites of the era by Ivory Joe Hunter, Chuck Willis, LaVern Baker, Bo Diddley, et al., but audiences were aware that always dangerous Tommy Lee Jones was ready to slither back

As very shady George Cole, always willing to separate gambler customers from their cash

Matt Dillon as J.C. "the Arm" Cullen playing up to a wary Tommy Lee Jones

onto the scene. It's Lee Grant's character who best sums him up for Cully: "George Cole is a rattlesnake. If you're smart, you'll stay away from him and his wife."

Variety's reviewer, "Adam.," concluded that "it is Tommy Lee Jones as the malevolent gangster with slicked-back hair, silk shirt and dollar-sign tie clip, who scowls and sneers his way through the scenes, easily stealing most he is in." He went on: "The ethics and morals of *The Big Town* are such that it could easily have been made in the '50s, and beneath all the gloss and glitz a simple tale is struggling to get out." Critic Roger Ebert gave the whole affair three and a half stars, called *The Big Town* "compulsively watchable not because of the plot, which is predictable down to the smallest detail,

but because of its acting, its direction and its style," and praised Tommy Lee Jones, in particular, "as the evil vice boss who has his best moments when he simply stands and looks at Dillon with eyes filled with hate."

The reviewer for *The Film Journal* called the film "a contrived, if flavorful, period piece," used the word "reptilian" in describing the Tommy Lee Jones character as he was played, and decided that "only Jones comes across as the lethal Cole, whose icy snarls and appearances from nowhere give *The Big Town* the sense of tough menace it desperately needs." And in the *New York Times*, critic Caryn James felt that "Tommy Lee Jones . . . doesn't have to do more than look sleazy and menacing."

Jones and the eclectic cast: (*clockwise*) Diane Lane, David Marshall
Grant, Matt Dillon, Suzy Amis, Bruce Dern, Lee Grant, and Tom
Skerritt, with Lane and Dillon in the center

14

STORMY MONDAY

ATLANTIC ENTERTAINMENT GROUP, 1988

CAST

Melanie Griffith (*Kate*), Tommy Lee Jones (*Francis Cosmo*), Sting (*Finney*), Sean Bean (*Brendan*), Alison Steadman (*Mayor*), Derek Hoxby (*Bob*), Mark Long (*Patrick*), James Cosmo (*Tony*), Andrzej Borkowski (*Andrej*), Dorota Zienska (*Christine*), Prunella Gee (*Mrs. Finney*), Heathcote Williams (*Peter Reed*), Catherine Chevalier (*Cosmo's secretary*), Richard Hawley (*Weegee's manager*), Caroline Hutchison (*Finney's secretary*), Roderic Leigh (*Councillor John Perry*), and Brian Lewis, Ying Tong John, Mick Hamer, Ian Hinchcliffe, Les Wilde, Dulice Liecier, Desmond Gill, Benny Graham, Brendan Philip Healey, Clive Curtis, Fiona Sloman, Elizabeth Mason, Tony Bluto, Don Weller, Andrew Cleyndert, Mark Taylor, Nick Pyne, Nicholas Lumley, Cy Benson, Keith Edwards, Louise Hobkinson, Guy Manning, Peter Marshall, Czeslaw Grocholski, Denny Ferguson, Billy Fellowes, Al Matthews.

CREDITS

A Film Four International production in association with the Movie Picture Company and British Screen. *Producer,* Nigel Stafford-Clark; *writer-director,* Mike Figgis; *cinematographer,* Roger Deakins; *production designer,* Andrew McAlpine; *music,* Mike Figgis; *editor,* Dave Martin. In color: *running time,* 93 minutes.

In this British-made neo–film noir thriller, toplined by American players Melanie Griffith and Tommy Lee

STORMY MONDAY (1988): As Cosmo, the devious American gangster, bent on making a real estate swindle in Newcastle, England

Jones, along with rock star turned actor Sting and an interesting new Irish actor, Sean Bean, Jones insinuatingly played a sharklike Texas businessman buying up waterfront property in Newcastle, England, for money-laundering purposes. Musician–fledgling filmmaker Mike Figgis (he not only wrote and directed the film but also scored it, much as John Carpenter does stateside) "has also gotten superb performances out of all four of his principals, who are fascinatingly mismatched" was the view of Janet Maslin of the *New York Times.* Moreover, "Mr. [Tommy Lee] Jones makes Cosmo dangerous in a much more direct way [than does costar Sting], and he turns the ugly-American role that is the screenplay's thinnest into much more than a mere caricature."

A stylish but rather nasty romance-*cum*-crime, rather vaguely scripted drama, which found a more receptive audience among film critics than moviegoers, *Stormy Monday* has a Yank real estate hustler named Cosmo limoing onto the scene with a couple of henchmen, trying to take over a small, depressed English town, beginning with a dingy waterfront jazz joint, the Key Club, owned by a hyperactive cat named Finney, and finds the town fathers quite receptive to his alluring advances. He's even arranged an "America Week" in town, with all the trappings and red, white, and blue bunting. "We're supposed to improve the quality of life, create jobs, and make lots of money," he tells "his people," one of whom is a seductive waitress named Kate, earlier secretly dispatched as sort of an advance girl to soften everyone up for the monetary kill. On the other hand, he makes no secret of his intention of having his goons rearrange Finney's face and renovate his fingers if he doesn't sell out to Cosmo. But Finney turns out to be a hard sell—matching Cosmo in his ruthlessness.

Into the mix early on comes an Irish drifter named Brendan (the film's unassuming hero), who asks for a job at Finney's place and soon becomes romantically involved with Kate. Overhearing two of Cosmo's thugs discussing ways of forcing Finney out, Brendan warns his boss, who sees to it that his own hired muscle are on hand. Hard-boiled Finney forces the thugs to sell their sports car to Brendan for a pound, breaks the arm of one of them, and makes certain that they are put aboard a London-bound train. Strong-arm give-and-take between Cosmo's gang and Finney's (usually offscreen) ensues until the two men come to an uneasy alliance, each having met his match, and turn their wrath on bad girl Kate and good guy Brendan following the latter's shooting of one of Cosmo's thugs. After arranging to have Kate leave with Brendan, Cosmo has a bomb planted in their car, set to explode at midnight. But the pair realize they've been set up and double back to the Key Club for a showdown with Cosmo. The absurd finale has Cosmo turning

on the charm after not long before having tried to blow up Kate and now offering to let her go off into the sunset with the hero ("Katie, you need a ride somewhere?" he asks her. "You're lucky I wasn't holding the gun, Cosmo," she tells him as Finney's men hold him at bay and usher him into a car); Brendan being dissuaded from shooting Cosmo; and Cosmo being driven out of town by the local bigwigs who earlier welcomed him and his money.

"The problem with *Stormy Monday*," noted Britain's *Monthly Film Bulletin*, "is that, in trying to be more than just a thriller, it winds up being not even a thriller. Typical of the trend is the film's simple inability to function in the seamless narrative terms of its Hollywood predecessors." In *Boxoffice*, on the other hand, there was a

terrific review for the film. "[The four leads] all give probably the best performances of their careers. And this is a great film . . . Jones is wonderfully loud and vicious as Cosmo, an avuncular Texan who seeks to buy, through any means available, as large a chunk of Newcastle as he can get away with. Cosmo may be, actually, the role Jones was born to play."

There was a diversity of other opinions. "Someday off in the future, when Tommy Lee Jones finally finds his way into a first-rate movie," critic Mike McGrady said in his three-star review in *New York Newsday*, "people will wonder where he's been all these years. Where he's been, mostly, is adding sinew to movies such as *Stormy Monday*, tough-minded flicks that are better than just so-

With a huge American flag as a backdrop (à la the opening scene of *Patton*), Jones prepares to charm the local council members in his "American Week" promotion and to boost business development.

Tommy Lee Jones and Sting—two bad dudes taking an outdoor meeting to discuss shady business

so but less than memorable." In *Newsweek*, David Denby felt that "the movie has an engagingly 'dark,' moody fatalism that is very pleasing" and that "Tommy Lee Jones is amusing as a vicious Mr. Big—an American financier trying to take over an English city." On the other side of the critical coin, this opinion came from "Lor." in *Variety:* "Tommy Lee Jones walks through his idiotic role with barely hidden embarrassment." Jones, it should be noted, played the gangster role as a tribute to tough screen guys of yore—puffing on foot-long cigars and using an imposing shiv to clean his fingernails while getting a point across to those he's scowling at.

Many of the critics found much to praise in the sleek photography of Roger Deakins and the soulful score by director Mike Figgis, obviously a jazz buff. The film itself was made entirely on location in Newcastle-Upon-Tyne.

15

THE PACKAGE

ORION PICTURES, 1989

CAST

Gene Hackman (*Johnny Gallagher*), Joanna Cassidy (*Eileen Gallagher*), Tommy Lee Jones (*Thomas Boyette*), Dennis Franz (*Milan Delich*), Reni Santoni (*Chicago police lieutenant*), Pam Grier (*Ruth Butler*), Chelcie Ross (*General Hopkins*), Ron Dean (*Karl Richards*), Kevin Crowley (*Walter Henke*), Thalmus Rasulala (*Secret Service commander*), Marco St. John (*Marth*), John Heard (*Col. Glen Whitacre*), Nathan Davis (*Soviet press secretary*), Joe Greco (*General Carlson*), Ike Pappas (*Himself*), and Michael Skewes, Johnny Lee Davenport, Juan Ramirez, Miguel Nino, Mik Scriba, Joe Guzaldo, Michael Tomlinson, Cody Glenn, Harry Lennix, Carlos Sanz, Diane Timmerman, Charles Mueller, Wilhelm von Homberg, Anthony Davydov, William Musyka, Gary Berkovich, Alex Hamilton, Greg Noonan, Harry Teinowitz, Don James, Gary Goldman, Katherine Lynch, Mary Siebel, Joe D. Lauck, Dick Cusack, Boris Leskin, Danny Goldring.

CREDITS

Executive producer, Arne L. Schmidt; *producers,* Beverly J. Cambe and Tobie Haggerty; *coproducers,* Andrew Davis and Dennis Haggerty; *director,* Andrew Davis; *screenplay,* John Bishop; *cinematographer,* Frank Tidy; *production designer,* Michael Levesque; *music,* James Newton Howard; *music director,* Marty Paich; *editors,* Don Zimmerman and Billy Weber. Deluxe color; *running time,* 108 minutes.

A "package" in military technospeak is a human commodity being transported from one place to another, generally unwillingly. Tommy Lee Jones, in this film, is "the Package," an enigmatic army sergeant in Germany who is being "escorted" back to the States to serve a prison sentence following a court-martial. Tough career noncom Gene Hackman has gotten the less than enviable escort assignment after having unwittingly fouled up a special-detail job while the United States was preparing for a historic armament conference in Berlin; his package was to be another soldier, who, he discovers en route, was switched. Seasoned Hackman and peevish Jones, on the journey back home, swap badinage in a verbal game of cat and mouse. ("You're quick, huh?" Jones, a cynic with a bad attitude, tells him during the somewhat tense trip. "This your wallet?" he asks, returning the lifted billfold). Upon arrival at the airport in Chicago, they find themselves split up in the men's room. In what at first appears to be a random brawl, Hackman is cornered and beaten up by a pair of thugs, and Jones takes off. Having lost his package, an angry Hackman heads for his prisoner's home locally, and there discovers, through family photographs, that he was escorting the wrong man. He has been set up and is determined not only to find out why but to retrieve the soldier who has escaped, Jones.

A professional warrior with a reputation to protect, Hackman reluctantly turns for help to his ex-wife, Joanna Cassidy, an army personnel officer who just hap-

THE PACKAGE (1989): In the title role as Boyette, the trained assassin. (photo: Deana Newcomb)

pens to be stationed in Chicago, and soon deduces that Jones was, in fact, a Vietnam veteran with a very shadowy past. When his original package's wife suddenly turns up dead, Hackman finds himself under house arrest for her murder, since he supposedly was the last one to see her alive. Then, when Cassidy's colleague is mysteriously gunned down and Cassidy herself may just be the next target of an unknown killer, he begins to suspect some sort of conspiracy but can't quite sort it out. A former Vietnam colleague now on the Chicago police force, Dennis Franz, leads him to a neo-Nazi group that might be tied in with the sinister but still unexplained plot in which Hackman finds himself.

Cassidy, meanwhile, has found herself trapped by the group and bundled off to a secluded hideout; there she is confronted by the missing Jones, who is preparing for an unnamed assignment. She is tied up, but after Jones leaves the next morning, she manages to free herself and breathlessly makes her way back to Hackman and Franz, who then get swallowed up in a crowd awaiting the arrival of American and Soviet leaders to celebrate the end of the cold war. Jones is then spotted on a rooftop with a

Tommy Lee Jones as the enigmatic "package" and Gene Hackman as the duped deliverer (photo: Deana Newcomb)

Hail fellows well met, minutes before Hackman loses "package" Jones

high-powered, scoped rifle. Hackman, quickly surveying the situation, comes to the conclusion that an assassination attempt is in the works. He then stumbles across the body of his original package, a dupe who had infiltrated the neo-Nazi group but was killed by Jones to shift suspicion in the shooting plot. Hackman races against time to quash the assassination and manages to face down Jones as he's about to fire on the Soviet leader. "Who pays you?" he demands of Jones. "*Everybody* pays me. I'm a public servant," Jones replies as Hackman guns him down. In the ensuing gunplay, the American army officer (John Heard) who initially had assigned Hackman his package and who, it turns out, was part of the conspiracy hatched by several renegade generals on both sides to protect each other's military complex in the emerging era of glasnost dies—shot by his own chauffeur, who is also under orders from those with their own agendas.

Third-billed Tommy Lee Jones (surprisingly, *after* Joanna Cassidy) refuses to be wiped off the screen in a role that requires him to say little and be absent from view for great stretches in this convoluted thriller—his first of several films for director Andrew Davis. Although Vincent Canby dismissed the movie out of hand in the

New York Times as "a feeble attempt to keep the old-fashioned cold-war thriller alive," *Variety*'s critic deemed it "smartly written and sharply played and directed at a pace that never sacrifices clarity for speed . . . an enormously satisfying political thriller. . . . In the brief but pivotal title role, [Tommy Lee] Jones shows it's possible to play an out-of-control psychopath without turning into a gargoyle." *Monthly Film Bulletin* commended it as an entertaining film and cited "an excellent performance by Jones." *People Weekly*'s Ralph Novak, on the other hand, chuckled that "Hackman, Jones and their costars . . . are such commanding actors that if you could hire them for an hour or so, they could make even your garage sale into a fairly entertaining project . . . although most garage sales have faster plots, more impressive action and snappier dialogue."

The Package was filmed on location in director Andrew Davis's native Chicago, as would be *The Fugitive*, reuniting Davis with Tommy Lee Jones. A trivia note: Among the players along with Jones in this film—and almost as sinister—was John Heard. Several years later, Heard would take the role in the television series of *The Client* that Jones created on the screen.

16
FIRE BIRDS

British Title: WINGS OF THE APACHE

BUENA VISTA/TOUCHSTONE PICTURES, 1990

CAST

Nicolas Cage (*Jack Preston*), Tommy Lee Jones (*Brad Little*), Sean Young (*Billie Lee Guthrie*), Bryan Kestner (*Breaker*), Dale Dye (*A. K. McNeil*), Mary Ellen Trainor (*Janet Little*), J. A. Preston (*General Olcott*), Peter Onorati (*Rice ["Riceman"]*), Charles Lanyer (*Darren Phillips*), Illana Shoshan (*Sharon Geller*), Marshall Teague (*Doug Daniels*), Cylk Cozart (*Dewar Proctor*), Charles Kahlenberg (*Oscar DeMarco*), Gregory Vahanian (*Tom Davis*), Bert Rhine (*Eric Stoller*) and Robert Lujan, Scott Williamson, Mickey Yablans, Peter Michaels, Richard Soto, Samuel Hernández, Kirstin Winn, Kristin Nicole Barnes, Phillip Troy, Harrison Le Duke, Garth Le Master, Judson Spense.

CREDITS

A Keith Barish/Arnold Kopelson production in association with Nova International Films. *Executive producers,* Arnold Kopelson and Keith Barish; *producer,* William Badalato; *director,* David Green; *screenplay,* Nick Theil and Paul F. Edwards, *from a story by* Step Tyner, John K. Swensson, and Dale Dye; *cinematographer,* Tony Imi; *aerial sequences,* Richard T. Stevens; *production designer,* Joseph T. Garrity; *music,* David Newman; *editors,* John Poll, Norman Buckley, and Dennis O'Connor. In Deluxe color; *running time,* 85 minutes.

In this unintentionally funny nineties updating of the old gung-ho World War II B movies and sophisticated helicopters replacing vintage prop planes of the time, *Fire Birds,* in the hands of British director David Green, managed to find itself critically panned on its release. Since the cold war was over and no enemy countries were around to be fought, the plot had to have the very well armed south-of-the-border drug cartel, working out of the "Catamarca Desert, South America" (as the audience is reminded by on-screen legends several times), as the politically popular enemy. Much of the early part of the less-than-engrossing, out-of-date propaganda piece dwelt on the advanced training of hotshot Apache helicopter pilots in the Arizona desert readying to take on the cartel.

Onto the scene strides impeccably credentialed and militarily correct Tommy Lee Jones, called to action as their instructor, rat-a-tat-tatting his air-force jargon in a style that would have made James Cagney proud. "You men know all there is to know—about air-to-ground technique," he informs his assembled copter squad in an almost dispassionate manner, giving equal emphasis to each and every word, "Starting right now you have a new objective in your lives, to become masters of air-to-air combat *tactics*. . . . When we have mastered these tactics we will use them to seek out and confront the forces of

Copter jocks Nicolas Cage and
Tommy Lee Jones

evil and kill them deader 'n hell." As a closer, he instructs them: "I expect you to improve every shining minute of my time by becoming *the* best air-to-air helicopter [he pronounces it "heel-o-copter"] pilots in the whole wide world." And anyone who knows a Tommy Lee Jones flick knows they damn well will be.

Fire Birds lifts not so subtly from such movies as *Apocalypse Now* (the stunning title sequence of copters flying toward the camera out of a setting-sun haze behind, following a precredit on-screen caution to drug cartels by George Bush!), *Top Gun* (cocky star Nicolas Cage swaggering in sky jock Tom Cruise's part), *An Officer and a Gentleman* (Cage being mentored by no-nonsense instructor Tommy Lee Jones), et al. And for political correctness there's even a lady combat pilot in the scrappy person of Sean Young to carry on an on-again, off-again romance and flying competition with Cage, promoting her feminist attitude but not missing a chance, when in the heat of battle and being pursued by an airborne bad guy, to plead with Cage, in another chopper: "Come on, Jake, save my ass!" Why, resourceful Sean even got the opportunity, in the heat of battle, after choppering in to save the wounded Tommy Lee, who'd crash-landed, to uncrate, assemble, and fire a stinger missile—despite the fact that she'd probably never seen one—and bring down the chief villain. At least she had Tommy Lee, still jammed into his cockpit and bleeding profusely, barking assembly instructions and encouragement.

Aside from the exceptional photography while aloft, the whole affair—straight out of a vintage Chester Morris–Richard Arlen combat-training movie five decades earlier—devolves to the nearly ludicrous, and one suspects that Tommy Lee Jones deliciously spits out his lines with such rapidity in order to get the whole enterprise wrapped up sooner than planned. At one point, he delights audiences and critics alike with a convoluted pep talk to prize student Cage, filled with non sequiturs that went something like: "Just like in the old war movies. You know, be a hero, that's what I'm looking for in you. First-class all-American hero with his heart and brain wired together cookin' full-tilt boogie for freedom and justice." And later, while being carted off on a stretcher at the finale, he repeats to crackerjack student Cage, "First-class all-American!"

"Tommy Lee Jones gets the call here," *USA Today* critic Mike Clark found, "not just to rough up South American drug cartels in a high-tech Apache helicopter, but also to deliver that choicest of lines [about 'full-tilt boogie'] from *Birds'* ruptured-duck script. . . . *Fire Birds* may actually be duller than Clint Eastwood's *Firefox*." In *The Cincinnati Enquirer*, reviewer Joe DeChick thought that "director David Green gets no help from Cage and

Young, who sleepwalk. Jones at least turns on his good-ol'-boy charm." And David Denby, in *New York* magazine, wrote: "*Fire Birds* is extremely short. I dare anyone to say anything more in its behalf." He ended his review with the observation that "the only watchable thing in the movie is Tommy Lee Jones, who runs through mili-

tary jargon so rapidly he appears to be turning it into a white boy's rap song."

The *New York Times*'s Vincent Canby considered *Fire Birds* "a ludicrous action-romance" and that "[it] had one director . . . two writers . . . and many laughs, all of them unintentional. Canby continued: "In roles that are almost nonexistent, [Tommy Lee] Jones and [Sean] Young are somewhat better than [Nicolas Cage]. He has a secure, cool manner that registers well on the screen, and she can be seen shouldering a portable, ground-to-air missile launcher . . . and knocking out an enemy jet. Mr. Jones and Miss Young don't have an easy time of it. Acting with Mr. Cage is a ruthless business. It's like sharing the screen with Cheetah."

FIRE BIRDS (1990): Instructor Tommy Lee Jones introduces his star pupil Nicolas Cage to feisty female chopper pilot Sean Young (*left*), unaware that they're old flames.

On one last training mission . . .

. . . and barking battle instructions after being downed

17

JFK

WARNER BROS., 1991

CAST

Kevin Costner (*Jim Garrison*), Sissy Spacek (*Liz Garrison*), Joe Pesci (*David Ferrie*), Tommy Lee Jones (*Clay Shaw*), Gary Oldman (*Lee Harvey Oswald*), Laurie Metcalf (*Susie Cox*), Michael Rooker (*Bill Broussard*), Jay O. Sanders (*Lou Ivon*), Gary Grubbs (*Al Oster*), John Candy (*Dean Andrews*), Jack Lemmon (*Jack Martin*), Walter Matthau (*Sen. Russell Long*), Ed Asner (*Guy Bannister*), Donald Sutherland (*Colonel "X"*), Dale Dye (*General "Y"*), Kevin Bacon (*Willie O'Keefe*), Brian Doyle-Murray (*Jack Ruby*), Sally Kirkland (*Rose Cehramie*), Beata Pozniak (*Marina Oswald*), Vincent D'Onofrio (*Bill Newman*), Tony Plana (*Carlos Bringuier*), Tomas Milan (*Leopoldo*), Wayne Knight (*Numa Bertel*), Tom Howard (*LBJ*), Jodie Farber (*Jackie Kennedy*), Ray LePere (*Zapruder*), Pruit Taylor Vince (*Lee Bowers*), Sean Stone (*Jasper Garrison*), Amy Long (*Virginia Garrison*), Scott Krueger (*Snapper Garrison*), Allison Pratt Davis (*Elizabeth Garrison*), Wayne Tippit (*FBI Agent Frank*), Jim Garrison (*Earl Warren*), and Bob Gunton, Anthony Ramirez, Steve Reed, Columbia Dubose, Randy Means, E. J. Morris, Cheryl Penland, Jim Gough, Perry R. Russo, Mike Longman, Alec Gifford, Pat Perkins, John William Galt, Ron Jackson, Red Mitchell, Raul Aranas, John C. Martin, Henri Alciatore, Willem Oltmans, Gail Cronauer, Roxie M. Franks, Zeke Mills, James N. Harrell, Ray Redd, Sally Nysteun, Jo Anderson, Marco Perella, Edwin Neal, Spain Logue, Darryl Cox, Carolina McCullogh, Chris Robinson, Melodee Bowman, Norman Davis, Linda Flores Wade.

CREDITS

An Ixtlan Corporation and A. Kitman Ho production in association with Le Studio Canal Plus, Regency Enterprises and Alcor Films. *Executive producer,* Arnon Milchan; *producers,* A. Kitman Ho and Oliver Stone; *coproducer,* Clayton Townsend; *director,* Oliver Stone; *screenplay,* Stone and Zachary Sklar, *based on the books* On the Trail of the Assassins *by* Jim Garrison *and* Crossfire: The Plot That Killed Kennedy *by* Jim Marrs; *cinematographer,* Robert Richardson; *production designer,* Victor Kempster; *music,* John Williams; *editors,* Joe Hutshing, Pietro Scalia, and Hank Corwin. DuArt color; *running time,* 189 minutes.

Contentious, controversial Oliver Stone made this personal "take" on the assassination of John F. Kennedy one of the most talked about films of the early nineties. Decidedly coming down on the conspiracy-theory argument, with several shooters hiding out on the infamous grassy knoll adjacent to Dealey Plaza in Dallas on that November day, *JFK*—a work of fiction that the producers were clear to stress—has as its focus Jim Garrison, then New Orleans district attorney, who makes his own conspiracy theory his obsession for the next two decades. Garrison, played tenaciously by Kevin Costner, takes exception (to say the least) to the Warren Commission Report, which found that Lee Harvey

Oswald had acted alone, and wends his way through the netherworld of right-wingers and other fanatics.

The road, as Garrison documents in his *On the Trail of the Assassins*—one of the books producer-director Stone used as the foundation for this expensive, expansive film—led him to several prominent gays who figured in the anti-Castro movement of the day, played in the film by Joe Pesci (in a dreadful toupee), Kevin Bacon, and especially Tommy Lee Jones, playing suave Louisiana businessman Clay Shaw, with snow-white hair. These are just three actors whose roles are threaded through an amazing cast of full-fledged stars and other lesser names—almost all of whom are seen only fleetingly. Even the real Jim Garrison has a part in the film—as Earl Warren, the Supreme Court justice who made the final judgment in the historical report that Garrison sets about to debunk!

Exuding an air of superiority, Tommy Lee Jones, not immediately recognizable, comes onto the scene well into the lengthy film—he's at first just a not-quite-in-focus background character—when Kevin Costner, as Garrison, tracks the movements of Lee Harvey Oswald (played by Gary Oldman) to pro-Castro demonstrations in New Orleans and to anti-Castroite Clay Shaw, well known to Garrison and a habitué of the city's gay demi-monde. Clay, Garrison comes to believe, is really a military intelligence agent sent to infiltrate fringe groups and has actually duped Oswald.

Garrison begins putting together, at least in his own mind, the whys and hows of the Kennedy assassination and ultimately sniffs around Washington, where supposed officials who prefer to be called only by single letters agree to meet with him in public places. The speculative "why" of the assassination is espoused by a

JFK (1991): Tommy Lee Jones as shady New Orleans businessman Clay Shaw meets with Kevin Costner, as D.A. Jim Garrison, and Michael Rooker (*center*) as Garrison's assistant.

White-haired Jones glowers menacingly at the trial at which Jim Garrison tries to link him to the assassination of John F. Kennedy.

The studio's pre-Oscar publicity to secure a nomination for
Tommy Lee Jones's performance

shadowy figure (who appears to be high in the military-industrial complex), played by Donald Sutherland in a lengthy monologue halfway into the picture set in the near-deserted mall opposite the Lincoln Memorial, with the Washington Monument conspicuous in the distance. Garrison becomes convinced that the Kennedy assassination was a coup d'état and that Shaw was one of its leading players. He returns to New Orleans and soon brings Shaw to trial. There Garrison, in his case against Shaw, sermonizes in the rambling, speculative "how" of the killing. Shaw merely sits at the defendant's table impassively, glowering occasionally and puffing away on his expensive cigarette holder. (Whether he was ever put on the stand is not alluded to in Stone's film.) Garrison is unable to convince a jury of Shaw's guilt—or even that there was a conspiracy—and seemingly loses his credibility. The jury, in truth, brings back a "not guilty" verdict in less than fifty minutes. Not mentioned by Stone is Garrison's continual attempts to drag Clay Shaw back into court on one charge or another tied in with the assassination until the federal courts put a stop to his efforts. An epilogue to the film informs the viewer that Clay Shaw died of lung cancer in 1974 and that Garrison went on to become a judge in New Orleans but never gave up trying to unmask the government "cover-up" over the years.

It is insightful to watch the screen pilferage of Jones, who, with limited dialogue and simple body English, rivets the viewer, particularly in the long courtroom scene during the film's last third as Kevin Costner is acting his tail off pleading his case. "Tommy Lee Jones is a powerful, if too overtly sinister, presence as Clay Shaw," David Ansen wrote in *Newsweek*. That weekly also concluded: "The problem with *JFK*—writ very large because it's a big movie with big stars about a big event—is the problem of the docudrama. A movie or a television show that re-creates history inevitably distorts history. It has to compress things into a short span; it has to extract clarity out of the essential messiness of life; it has to abide by certain dramatic conventions. . . . All this makes for exag-

geration. In *JFK* all these problems are compounded by taking a highly speculative version of events—the Garrison/Stone conspiracy theory—and grafting it onto real events."

Most of the other reviewers fell into two camps—pro and con. There seemed to be no middle ground. "A masterpiece . . . the best movie of the year," Roger Ebert said in the *Chicago Sun-Times*. "A rebuke to official history and a challenge to continue investigating the crime of the century, Oliver Stone's *JFK* is electric, muckraking filmmaking," *Variety* wrote. "This massive, never-boring political thriller, which most closely resembles Costa-Gavras' *Z* in style and impact, lays out just about every shred of evidence yet uncovered for the conspiracy-theory argument. . . ." And in the view of Vincent Canby (*New York Times*), "*JFK,* for all its sweeping innuendos and splintery music-video editing, winds up breathlessly but running in place. . . . [It] begins with a promise of intrigue and revelation, though it soon becomes clear that [Oliver] Stone is Fibber McGee opening the door to an overstuffed closet. . . . What is fact and what isn't is not easy to tell."

An Academy Award nomination for Best Supporting Actor came Tommy Lee's way for his portrayal of Shaw. (*Variety* called it "superbly smooth.") It was one of eight for the film (including Best Picture, Best Director, and Best Screenplay). Jones lost out to Jack Palance on Oscar night, and *JFK* ended up with just two statuettes—for cinematography and film editing. The film, about which Stone was so passionate, never really captured the consciousness of the public—other than the true believers—and he turned his passion to his next project, *Heaven and Earth,* another of his Vietnam cinematic statements, and the one after that, the landmark *Natural Born Killers.* Tommy Lee Jones had significant roles in both of those films.

In 1993, Stone's "director's cut" version of *JFK* was released on video with an additional seventeen minutes of "lost" footage, including at least one extra scene featuring Tommy Lee Jones as Clay Shaw.

18

UNDER SIEGE

WARNER BROS., 1992

CAST

Steven Seagal (*Casey Rybeck*), Tommy Lee Jones (*William Strannix*), Gary Busey (*Commander Krill*), Erika Eleniak (*Jordan Tate*), Patrick O'Neal (*Captain Adams*), Nick Mancuso (*Tom Breaker*), Andy Romano (*Admiral Bates*), Damian Chapa (*Tackman*), Troy Evans (*Granger*), David McNight (*Flicker*), Lee Hinton (*Cue Ball*), John Ruttger (*Commander Green*), Brad Rea (*Marine guard*), Michael Welden (*Lieutenant Ballard*), Bernie Casey (*Commander Harris*), Raymond Cruz (*Ramirez*), Michael Des Barres (*Damiani*), Duane Davis (*Johnson*), Colm Meaney (*Daumer*), Dennis Lipscomb (*Trenton*), Dale Dye (*Captain Garza*), and Rickey Pierre, Eddie Bo Smith Jr., Richard Jones, Tom Reynolds, Tom Muila, Tom Wood, Jerome Wiggins, Joseph F. Kosala, Robert Nichols, Joseph R. John, Conrad E. Palmisano, Luis J. Silva, Daniel H. Friedman, Bruce Bozzi, Sandy Ward, Nate Robinson, Gary Gardner, Craig A. Pinkard.

CREDITS

An Arnon Michan production, in association with Le Studio Canal Plus, Regency Enterprises and Alcor Films. *Executive producers*, J. F. Lawton and Gary Goldstein; *producers*, Arnon Milchan, Steven Seagal, and Steven Reuther; *coproducers*, J. B. Bernstein and Peter Macgregor-Scott; *director*, Andrew Davis; *screenplay*, J. F. Lawton; *cinematographer*, Frank Tidy; *production designer*, Bill Kenney; *music*, Gary Chang; *editors*, Robert A. Ferretti, Dennis Virkler, Don Brochu, and Dov Hoenig. Technicolor and Panavision; *running time*, 102 minutes.

At his maddest, Tommy Lee Jones cuts a swath through *Under Siege*—sort of a *Die Hard* on the high seas—as a nuclear pirate, conspiring to steal warheads from a U.S. battleship, unaware at first that he's run afoul of Steven Seagal, a disgraced ex-navy SEAL and Vietnam vet working out his days to retirement as a cook below deck. Then, of course, Jones begins to relish the cat-and-mouse game he's forced into as slow-to-anger Seagal attempts to take back the ship that Jones has hijacked. Jones, as William Strannix, in the guise of a leather-clad rock musician in an unauthorized helicopter, has boarded the USS *Missouri*, together with a stripper and an entourage of "caterers," for a surprise birthday party for the skipper (played by Patrick O'Neal). At around the same time, the ship's turncoat executive officer, Krill (Gary Busey), has a run-in with Casey Rybeck (Seagal) in the galley and has him placed under guard in a meat locker off the mess area. Krill then kills the skipper in his cabin, and Strannix takes over the vessel, ordering the remaining crew into a secured, locked area. Before disabling the onboard satellite system, Strannix, a crazed renegade agent, alerts his former CIA boss in Washington that he has the launch codes for the nuclear missiles and that he intends to offload them after possibly nuking Honolulu and to sell them for $100 million. Krill, who has thrown in with him, is not as efficient as

Strannix would like, it turns out, and causes him a number of unexpected problems.

Rybeck not long afterward manages to free himself, still unaware that the ship has been hijacked, and soon finds the skipper's body and then stumbles upon the terrified Jordan Tate (Erika Eleniak, the one female in the mix). It seems she has missed out on all of the shooting by Strannix and cohorts, having fallen asleep inside the cake, out of which she was scheduled to pop; when she finally did, she found a dead crew all around her. Reluctantly taking her along as his sidekick, Rybeck begins his search for the terrorist, moving up and down between decks, destroying Strannix's helicopter, killing several of his associates, and ultimately freeing the crew that has been herded into the ship's forecastle and threatened with drowning when Strannix has the sprinkler system turned on. While thwarting Strannix at every turn, Rybeck slowly and rather violently closes in on his prey. Strannix does, though, manage to decimate a squad of Navy SEALS dispatched to the ship by the Pentagon, at the same time that Rybeck is single-handedly decimating Strannix's gang of cutthroats. The showdown takes place in the ship's computer room, where, in a fight obligatory in every Steven Seagal flick, he does great bodily harm to his villainous costar—jamming his thumb into Tommy Lee's eye socket, stabbing him through the top of his skull with a butcher knife, and then slamming his head into a plugged-in radar screen.

The de rigueur mayhem aside, along with Seagal's one-note acting, the joy for the viewer is relishing Tommy Lee Jones's nutcake routine. Making his initial appearance in shades, leather jacket, headband, and large crosses dangling from his neck (he introduces himself and his cronies to the crew as Bad Billy and the Bailjumpers), Jones immediately takes charge. "Four minutes ahead of schedule—damn, I'm good!" Then he begins barking orders, lapping up every moment. "You know, I missed the sixties."

Just before the showdown, Jones engages Seagal—both represent two sides of the same coin as disaffected and disgruntled military men—in some verbal sparring in their only face-to-face encounter. Prowling around with a pistol, Jones tells his adversary: "Step over there. You're gonna watch the end of the world on television, my man. Put your feet up. Relax. You know, you're good—you are really good. It's gonna be a shame to kill you." Then, pointing to his charts and computer screens, he says, "Behold my finest work." Seagal responds, "Tell me—you really think blowing up a bunch of innocent people is gonna change anything? Who made you flip like that?" Jones: "I got tired of coming up with last-minute, desperate solutions to impossible problems created by other people." Seagal: "All of your ridiculous,

pitiful antics aren't going to change a thing. You and I, we're puppets in the same sick play. We serve the same master, and he's a lunatic and he's ungrateful, and there's nothing we can do about it. You and I—we're the same." Jones: "Oh, no—no, no, no—there's a difference, my man. You have faith—I don't."

The huge-grossing *Under Siege* was the second of three films Jones did with director Andrew Davis, who admitted, "The part was written for Elton John. Tommy wanted to do it as Alice Cooper. We compromised on Paul Butterfield." The *New York Times*'s Vincent Canby thought that the film was "just lunatic enough to keep you watching the screen while snorting in uncertain derision. The movie prompts awe and out-of-control laughter, but who is sending up whom?" He also felt that "Mr.

Jones had a lot of fun as the mad brains of the hijacking operation." In *People,* meanwhile, critic Ralph Novak said: "An old-fashioned, all-nonsense action adventure, this is not, to damn it with faint praise, Seagal's worst movie. It is fast and colorful enough to be a James Bond film, assuming the Bond humor failed to show up. . . . Villains [Tommy Lee] Jones and [Gary] Busey swagger all over the place trying to keep Seagal from thwarting their evil plans. Jones, especially, makes a convincing psycho."

The New Yorker commented that "the novelty of casting Seagal as a dangerous cook tickles his fans and at least keeps non-fans open-minded. But once [he] drops his disguise the movie's biggest joke evaporates," also saying that "Tommy Lee Jones, who gives the best performance in the movie, comes up with a surprise or two: when he's not being comically casual, he spoofs his own intensity." And this from *Variety:* "Scoring again after his Oscar-nominated role in *JFK,* Jones forcefully portrays a deranged villain, and looks great in black leather jacket and sunglasses. . . . The anticipated climax, a man-to-man fight between Seagal and Jones, is not only long in coming, but also too brief and disappointingly staged."

In the summer of 1995, Seagal reprised his hero role in the much less potent set-aboard-a-train sequel (or rather reworking) called *Under Siege 2: Dark Territory,* which lacked a pivotal element in such thrillers: a dynamic villain. Unfortunately for the producers, Tommy Lee Jones had been killed off in the original.

UNDER SIEGE (1992): Garbed as a rock star, Jones is deranged ex-Special Forces leader William Strannix, taking over the ship and crew on the USS *Missouri* .

Planning his attack with Gary Busey, as corrupt naval commander
Krill, on learning that Steven Seagal is still onboard and
roaming free

Strannix lays out his shipboard demands to defense bigwigs in Washington.

Hot-tempered Strannix will brook no dissent to his maniacal plan.

Jones goes mano a mano with Seagal in the climactic showdown in the ship's computer room.

19

HOUSE OF CARDS

PENTA PICTURES/MIRAMAX FILMS, 1993

CAST

Kathleen Turner (*Ruth Matthews*), Tommy Lee Jones (*Dr. Jake Beerlander*), Park Overall (*Lillian Huber*), Asha Menina (*Sally Matthews*), Shiloh Strong (*Michael Matthews*), Esther Rolle (*Adelle*), Michael Horse (*Stoker*), Anne Pitoniak (*Judge*), Jacqueline Cassel (*Gloria Miller*), Joaquin Martinez (*Sceteral*), John Henderson (*Bart Huber*), Craig Fuller (*Roy Huber*), Rick Marshall (*Frank Stearson*), Reuben Valiquette Murray (*Reuben*), Emily Russell (*Emily*), and Joseph Michael Sipe Jr., Yvette Thor, Connie Washburn, Samuel David Miller, Michael McDaniel, Robert W. Lyon, Luchena Huntley, Isaac J. Banks, Eric Coble, John Bennes, Nick Searcy, Lloyd Barcroft.

CREDITS

Presented by Mario & Vittorio Cecchi Gori and Silvio Berlusconi, in association with A&M Films. *Executive producer,* Vittorio Cecchi Gori; *co-executive producer,* Gianni Nunnari; *producers,* Dale Pollock, Lianne Halfon, and Wolfgang Glattes; *coproducer,* Jonathan Sanger; *writer-director,* Michael Lessac; *based on a story by* Lessac and Robert Jay Lutz; *cinematographer,* Victor Hammer; *production designer,* Peter Larkin; *music,* James Horner; *editor,* Walter Murch. Technicolor; *running time,* 108 minutes.

In this enigmatic drama Tommy Lee Jones is a bespectacled child psychologist who comes into the life of widowed architect Kathleen Turner and her two young children, played by Shiloh Strong and a remarkable little girl named Asha Menina, after the girl mysteriously stops talking and retreats into her own strange world. "Beerlander. Jacob T. Beerlander," he introduces himself to Ruth Matthews (Turner), who has gone into denial when her six-year-old daughter Sally begins exhibiting classic autistic syndrome upon the family's return from a Mexican dig during which her architect daddy has been killed (offscreen). Jake has shown up at their house to find Ruth in a precarious position after having climbed out onto the roof when she spots no-longer-verbal Sally fearlessly walking along the leaf-filled gutter to retrieve her older brother's baseball. After rescuing both Ruth and Sally, Jake patiently observes the mother trying to communicate with her daughter. "Mrs. Matthews. When'd your little girl stop talking." (As in many of his films, Jones appears to make declarative statements out of questions and doesn't talk with question marks.)

Pooh-poohing the situation, Ruth at first sends Dr. Jake on his way, but little by little she watches her daughter slowly enter a world of her own, one night finding that Sally has created a complex structure out of old family photos and tarots and regular playing cards—the house of cards of the title. Grabbing a camera, Ruth takes a series of pictures before accidentally knocking the whole thing over. She shows Jake what Sally has created, piquing his interest even further. She then reluctantly turns Sally over to Jake for observation but hovers over her despite Jake's protestations. Ruth becomes involved with the parent of another autistic child at Jake's medical facility and with several of the children there, "linking" with them—breaking into their private world that has allowed them a remarkable math ability (as demonstrated by Dustin Hoffman as an autistic adult in *Rain Man* in 1988). Learning of Ruth's meddling, Jake goes ballistic, screaming at her: "You linked. You linked into their world. That's wonderful! Why don't you just time-warp back into mine, please! Jesus, think you're the first person to see God in the face of a hurt child?" His wrath continues: "I have lived with these children twenty years. Every morning I wake up praying that one of them, just one, would do a single, stupid, dim-witted thing like tie your shoes or throw your arms around your mom. When's the last time Sally did that? Just threw her arms around you? Why aren't you fighting for that? Miracles wear awfully thin around here, Mrs. Matthews. Normal is awesome." (Don't try figuring out what this mishmash of a monologue is meant to mean.)

Ruth continues to maintain her high-pressure architectural job while trying to renew verbal contact with Sally. But then there's a terrifying incident when, while accompanying her mom to a skyscraper site which Ruth

is overseeing, Sally, apparently in her own world, climbs a skeletal frame and walks out unafraid onto a high beam in order to reach the moon, where a shaman from the family's last days in Mexico has told her that her father now resides. Following Sally's rescue, Ruth is hauled into social-services court by Jake and has her daughter taken from her. An arrangement is struck by which Sally can spend nights in her own bed and compassionate Jake will have her during the day so that he can continue his observations. "My God, little girl, where are you taking us all?" he privately asks as he watches her do her thing in her own world. Ruth, meanwhile, computer-designs and then, hoping to reach Sally, constructs a massive spiral structure in her multiacred backyard

that mirrors the house of cards she had seen in Sally's room.

Like the real house of cards, the film at this point begins crumbling in its rush to a less than satisfying ending as Ruth drags and coaxes Sally up this spiraling yellow brick road as Jake watches, speechless. Mother and daughter miraculously make contact, and Sally returns to her preautistic days and ways.

House of Cards emerged as a project that seems to have escaped from the small screen—a low-key, intimate film with lots of close-ups. It was constructed, apparently, as a story from the doctor's viewpoint, but when a somewhat blowzy Kathleen Turner became attached to the production, the decision was made to shift the spotlight to her character. The film, made in late 1991 by the Italian consortium known as Penta Pictures for release by Twentieth Century-Fox, was abandoned when several other Penta productions did poorly at the box office, and it took eighteen months before a distributor could be found and it premiered at Robert Redford's Sundance Institute, at a film festival in February 1993. *House of Cards* was dismissed by most critics as an interesting but flawed attempt by writer and first-time director Michael Lessac. Vincent Canby in the *New York Times* wrote: "Nothing quite makes sense. [Tommy Lee] Jones has no role. He wears a lot of white shirts and a concerned expression." In *Newsday*, critic John Anderson observed that "Jones, whose patient, dedicated Jake

Pondering the impenetrable after meeting the autistic youngster: why she stopped talking

117

should have been the hero of the piece, has his legs cut from under him by an absurdly contrived ending and a mentality that reduces a child's mental illness to a dramatic device." And critic Desson Howe, in the *Washington Times,* thought that "Jones has chosen the wrong project to slide out of his familiar bad-boy villain-ous roles. There's so little to work with. He's just a sensitive doctor full of Freudian assertions and menschlike patience, a genial abstraction in a white coat."

Ironically, Jones came to this project directly after working on another one that also would not show up on a movie screen for a number of years, *Blue Sky.*

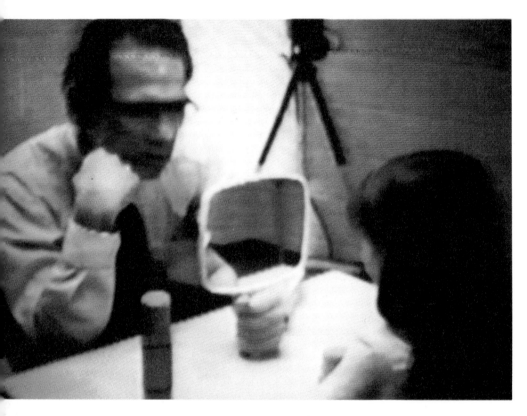

Doctor and patient: attempting to break through

THE FUGITIVE (1993): As U.S. marshal Sam Girard, arriving at the train-wreck scene from which Dr. Richard Kimble, convicted wife killer, has made his escape

20

THE FUGITIVE

WARNER BROS., 1993

CAST

Harrison Ford (*Dr. Richard Kimble*), Tommy Lee Jones (*Marshal Samuel Gerard*), Sela Ward (*Helen Kimble*), Julianne Moore (*Dr. Anne Eastman*), Joe Pantoliano (*Cosmo Renfro*), Andreas Katsulas (*Frederick Sykes*), Jeroen Krabbé (*Dr. Charles Nichols*), Daniel Roebuck (*Biggs*), L. Scott Caldwell (*Poole*), Ron Dean (*Detective Kelly*), Joseph Kosala (*Detective Rosetti*), Tom Wood (*Newman*), Dick Cusack (*Walter Guthrie*), Richard Riehle (*Old guard*), Andy Romano (*Judge Bennett*), Nick Searcy (*Sheriff Rawlins*), Eddie Bo Smith Jr. (*Copeland*), Miguel Nino and Tony Fosco (*Chicago cops*), Joseph F. Fisher (*Otto Sloan*), James Liautuad (*Paul*), David Darlow (*Dr. Alexander Lentz*), and Tom Galouzis, James F. McKinsey, Mark D. Espinoza, John E. Ellis, Gene Barge, Thomas C. Simmons, Joseph Guzaldo, Nick Kusenko, Joan Kohn, Joe D. Lauck, Joseph V. Gustaferro, Thom Vernon, Ken Moreno, Frank Ray Perilli, Otis Wilson, Pancho Dennings, Danny Goldring, Jim Wilkey, Kevin Crowley, Michael Skewes.

CREDITS

A Keith Barish/Arnold Kopelson production. *Executive producer,* Roy Huggins; *producer,* Arnold Kopelson; *coproducer,* Peter MacGregor-Scott; *director,* Andrew Davis; *screenplay,* Jeb Stuart and David Twohy, *from a story by* Twohy *based on characters created by* Huggins; *cinematographer,* Michael Chapman; *production designer,* Dennis Washington; *music,* James Newton Howard; *editors,* Dennis Virkler, David Finfer, Dean Goodhill, Don Brochu, Richard Nord, and Dov Hoenig. Technicolor; *running time,* 127 minutes.

Being suddenly confronted by his quarry in a giant sewer tunnel

120

"*The Fugitive* is in for one hell of a run," *Variety* led off its rave review. "The movie . . . is a giant toy-train entertainment with all stops pulled out. A consummate nail-biter that never lags, it leaves you breathless from the chase yet anxious for the next bit of mayhem or clever plot twist." Among the 1990s big-screen versions of memorable television series of the past, *The Fugitive* arguably was the best; in fact, it was even better than the 1963–67 David Janssen series that most fans and TV classicists recall. It was twenty-five years from the time Janssen stopped running after 120 episodes when box-office hero Harrison Ford took up the death-defying race, determined, after making a breathtaking escape while on his way to prison, having been framed for the killing, to find the one-armed man who murdered his wife. Tommy Lee Jones becomes his dogged pursuer, yapping at his heels—intent on clapping the escaped fugitive back behind bars, not necessarily to help solve the killing, of which his quarry proclaims innocence.

The initial setup, as in the series, has Ford, as Richard Kimble, a prominent Chicago surgeon, returning home to find his wife murdered but in time to struggle with a one-armed man he has discovered lurking in his house. Knocked out, Kimble is found and interrogated by the police, becomes the prime suspect in the killing, goes to trial on circumstantial evidence, is found guilty, and re-ceives the death sentence. On his way to prison, the bus in which he is shackled to other rebellious convicts is involved in a miniriot. The driver loses control of the vehicle, which rolls down an embankment onto a set of railroad tracks. Kimble, as a doctor, is freed from his shackles by a guard so that he can minister to the wounded but quickly becomes aware that a speeding freight train is hurtling down on them. In one of the great film set pieces of modern cinema, he manages to leap from the overturned bus with another prisoner as the train crashes into it in a spectacular derailment.

After the crash it's desperate Dr. Kimble on the run, with the law, represented by Deputy Marshal Gerard (Jones), in relentless pursuit. Ford actually has little to say for much of the rest of the film. He continues to flee, doing his patented anxious, grim-faced, lump-in-the-throat characterization, occasionally changing his appearance (he's bearded at the beginning of the movie) and outfits when the convenient moment arises. He turns up in the most improbable places after surviving an incredible dive into a dam after an early encounter with his chief pursuer, who has become Inspector Javert to his Jean Valjean in this unabashed twist on Victor Hugo's *Les Misérables*, right down to the hunter hounding the prey through a storm drain. Once he comes onto the scene as Gerard, begins barking orders to his men, and

After losing his man, Girard marshals assistants Renfro (Joe Pantoliano, *left*) and Biggs (Daniel Roebuck) to press the search.

Tommy Lee Jones as the relentless marshal

takes the case of the missing prisoners away from local authorities and makes it his own, Tommy Lee Jones sears his own brand into the film (his third with director Andrew Davis, after *The Package* and *Under Siege*). "MY, MY, MY, MY, MY . . . WHAT A MESS!" he says on first seeing the crash site, with typical Tommy Lee emphasis on every word. "We're always fascinated when we find leg irons with no legs in them," he says to his four associates. "Your fugitive's name is Dr. Richard Kimble. Go get him!" The methodical but indefatigable Gerard not long afterward traps Kimble in a viaduct and confronts him for the first of only two times in the film. Kimble, who has gotten the drop on Gerard, both standing ankle-deep in water,

tells his pursuer, "I didn't kill my wife!" To which Gerard replies, "I don't care." (Gerard would later explain that his sole job was to recapture Kimble, not judge him or even solve what might have been a miscarriage of justice.) But as Gerard moves in on him, Kimble knows he's trapped, since the viaduct opens on to a huge dam hundreds of feet below. Seeing no other way out, Kimble jumps and is swept away in the raging torrent below.

Gerard, who will remain unconvinced that his prey is dead until he sees a lifeless body, presses on with his search. He calls in dogs and helicopters to scour the area. "Sam, are you out of your mind?" one of his team asks. "The man is dead." Gerard's comeback: "That'll make him easier to catch." And then, as he thanks the local authorities for the use of the bloodhounds, he regroups and barks to his colleagues, "Operation ain't over until the big dog howls. . . . So he showed up not dead yet. Let that be a lesson to you. Never argue with the big dog. Big dog is always right!" The trail eventually leads back to Chicago, Kimble's home turf, where he is determined to clear his name. With memories of his wife in a pool of blood and a one-armed man racing out the front door, he begins to snoop first around the hospital where he had worked (here he manages to to surreptitiously save the life of a young patient), looking for information on protheses for amputation victims, and then the courthouse hall of records for data on accident amputees. Literally steps behind Kimble, Gerard nearly catches up with his quarry, but he loses him in a St. Patrick's Day parade, another of the film's terrific set pieces.

Kimble's desperate search leads him inexorably to the one-armed man (that's the "who" of the puzzle, which is basically where the TV series ended). He, it turns out, is an ex-cop turned contract hit man, leading Kimble next to the "why" of the puzzle. Kimble makes telephone contact with Gerard and reminds him of the brief conversa-tion they had in the tunnel when they faced each other down. "I don't care," Gerard repeats himself. "I'm not try-ing to solve a puzzle." Kimble's comeback: "Well, I am—and I found a big piece." He soon discovers that the one-armed man is stalking him, and there is a shoot-out on a Chicago El train. The motorman is killed, and Kimble subdues his quarry, handcuffing him to a post on the train and then running once again before Gerard and the city's transit police can nab him.

Putting the pieces together, Kimble makes his way to a downtown hotel where a medical convention is in progress, and he confronts an old colleague, Charles Nichols (Jeroen Krabbé, the film's second villain), who, it turns out, has become involved in a pharmaceutical scam involving drugs which Kimble had been testing, and wanted Kimble out of the way. The two have a furi-ous fight over several floors of the hotel as Gerard and his men close in. "Richard, I'm either lying or I'm gonna shoot you. What do you think?" Gerard tells Kimble after cornering him. However, Nichols attacks with a lead pipe, and the battle moves to the roof of the hotel. Kimble manages to save the life of Gerard, who finally admits that the man he has been chasing really is inno-

Deep in thought and piecing things together after finding his trail leads to prosthetics department of a Chicago hospital .

cent. "It's over now. You know, I'm glad. I need the rest," Gerard admits to Kimble. Finally vindicated, Kimble allows himself to be taken back into custody. As he and Gerard get into the back of a squad car, Kimble says to him: "I thought you didn't care." Gerard replies: "I don't—but don't tell anybody, okay?"

While the film's hero did all the running and sweating and working furiously (as in *JFK* previously), Tommy Lee Jones ended up with the more interesting (if not meatier) role—and this time he walked off with the Oscar as Best Supporting Actor for his performance as Deputy Marshal Sam Gerard. Britain's *Sight and Sound* noted: "*The Fugitive* is a remarkably successful Hollywood product with a brilliantly contrived star double act pursuing different paths through the central plot." It also observed: "The most interesting character, as in the series, is Gerard; while Barry Morse's [television] cop was a near-psychotic loner, Jones' marshal is surrounded by a Hawksian team he alternately cajoles and abuses with a delightful stream of patter. It is Gerard's professionalism which keeps him on the case when the quarry is almost certainly dead . . . and forces him finally to concede not only that Kimble is innocent but that his innocence matters." And this rave from Janet Maslin (*New York Times*): "As directed sensationally by Andrew Davis and acted to steely perfection by Harrison Ford, Tommy Lee Jones and a flawless cast it is a film whose every element conspires to sustain crisp intelligence and a relentless pace. . . . To put it simply, this is a home run."

It should be noted that the success of *The Fugitive* in multiplexes around the country prompted NBC to make a most unusual programming decision: to dust off the two-hour series finale (which for many years was the highest-rated television event ever when initially shown on August 29, 1967) and rerun it a quarter century later in prime time—to very respectable ratings.

Tommy Lee Jones was scheduled to reprise his role of Marshal Sam Gerard in 1996 in a sequel to this film called *U.S. Marshals*.

Having his man in his sights

21

HEAVEN AND EARTH

WARNER BROS., 1993

CAST

Tommy Lee Jones (*Sgt. Steve Butler*), Joan Chen (*Mama*), Haing S. Ngor (*Papa*), Hiep Thi Le (*Le Ly*), Dustin Nguyen (*Sau*), Debbie Reynolds (*Eugenia*), Conchata Ferrell (*Bernice*), Vivian Wu (*Madame Lien*), Thuan K. Nguyen (*Uncle Luc*), Liem Whatley (*Viet Cong captain*), Michael Paul Chan (*Interrogator*), Dale Dye (*Larry*), Timothy Carhart (*Big Mike*), Kevin Gallagher (*Tall Marine*), Bussaro Sanruck (*Le Ly, age five*), and Thaun Le, Supak Pititam, Lan Nguyen Calderon, Mai Le Ho, Vinh Dang, Khiem Thai, Michelle Vynh Le, Tuan Tuan, Aron Starrat, Peter Duong, Hieu Van Vu, Michael Lee, Irene Ng, Truc-Hanh Tran, Robert John Burke, Timothy Guinee, Brian Helnick, Scott Berwill, Annie McEnroe, Marianne Muellerleile, Marshall Bell.

CREDITS

An Ixtlan/Regency Enterprises production in association with Le Studio Canal Plus, Alcor Films. Todd-AO/TAE. *Executive producer,* Mario Kassar; *producers,* Oliver Stone, Arnon Milchan, Robert Kline, and A. Kitman Ho; *coproducer,* Clayton Townsend; *writer-director,* Oliver Stone; *based on the books* When Heaven and Earth Change Places *by* Le Ly Hayslip, with Jay Wurts, *and* Child of War, Woman of Peace *by* Le Ly Hayslip, with James Hayslip; *cinematographer,* Robert Richardson; *production designer,* Victor Kempster; *music,* Kitaro; *editors,* David Brenner and Sally Menke. Technicolor and Panavision; *running time,* 140 minutes.

Oliver Stone turned to Vietnam for the third time for this beautifully told, if lengthy, tale based on the forty-year personal saga of Le Ly Hayslip, a beleaguered peasant woman who endures the war first as a child under the French and then a teenager in servitude in Saigon in the early 1960s. Along the way there is brutalization by the Republican army, rape and torture by the Viet Cong, exploitation and disgrace by her "big city" master for whom she has become a servant, and finally a not-so-ideal marriage to an unstable GI and her attempts to assimilate into the land of the great shopping mall. The entire film rests on the delicate shoulders of an unknown actress, Hiep Thi Le, and although he receives top billing, Tommy Lee Jones does not make an appearance until more than halfway through the long film, and then for only limited footage. His character, the gentle (at first) GI traumatized by 'Nam, the heroine's savior who becomes increasingly violent when the two are stateside, is actually a composite of American men in the life of Le Ly Hayslip, whose autobiographical books formed the basis of the Oliver Stone epic-sized script.

Le Ly escapes the turmoil of the midland villagers and finds her way to Da Nang, where her older sister has be-

HEAVEN AND EARTH (1993): As Marine sergeant Steve Butler (photo: Roland Neveu)

come a whore, tossed out of her house as a tramp when she tried to return to her family. It is on the streets of Saigon where Le Ly, now with a young son by her "master," is saved from several predatory American soldiers by a quiet, reclusive GI named Steve Butler (a subdued Tommy Lee Jones), who "just needs someone to talk to." A romance of sorts develops between the two, and he compulsively proposes, offering to take her away from all this for the good life in America. "I know all about karma. My karma has taken me all over this world most of my life, livin' out of a duffel bag," Steve tells her in a private moment. "And that's why I'm here. It's time for me to settle down and quit pretendin' I'm gonna live forever. I'm goin' home . . . to San Diego. I got a house, family there, and I want you to be there with me. You'll be safe. You'll be free. Your boy'll have his freedom and an education. My first wife taught me a real lesson in my life. I'm serious. *I need a good* Oriental woman, like you, if you'll have me." It will be another three years before this can happen. Back in the States, Le Ly finds herself and her son adrift in an alien culture. Accepted by Steve's sister and mother (Debbie Reynolds, in her first movie in two decades), she and Steve have two more sons. "This is America, baby," he has bragged to her. "The store stays open twenty-four hours. You don't need money in America." Handing her a check, he tells her, "You just give this piece of paper to the store, and the bank pays it." But things have turned sour for him, and he becomes increasingly withdrawn and angered by his failure in various civilian enterprises, like gunrunning, and takes that anger out on her ever more frequently. Meanwhile, Le Ly has become self-sufficient, making her way up the economic ladder. Steve finally implodes and kidnaps her children. In despair, he strips naked in a van and commits suicide.

Cut to thirteen years later: the resilient Le Ly, now a successful eighties American businesswoman, returns to Vietnam to introduce her older son to his father and then to look up her family back in her village. Her brother scorns her capitulation to capitalism, but her aged, long-suffering mother (the lovely Joan Chen, dressed down and uglied up as a toothless peasant) expresses pride in what Le Ly has become, while in a dream Le Ly also senses approval from her long-dead father (Haing S. Ngor, the Oscar-winning Cambodian actor from *The Killing Fields*). Sadly she accepts her destiny never to be wholly Vietnamese or American but somewhere between Father Heaven, *Ong Troi,* and Mother Earth, *Me Dat.* "Between Heaven and Earth, *Troi va Dat,* are the people," the film's prologue has said, "striving to bring forth the harvest and follow Lord Buddha's teachings."

Most critics found Tommy Lee Jones's role—from good guy to unstable monster in a single reel—some-

Tommy Lee Jones puts in his first appearance midway into the film surveying the situation in downtown Saigon.
(photo: Roland Neveu)

what hard to swallow until it became clear that his part was made up of several men in Le Ly's life. Janet Maslin wrote in the *New York Times:* "Certainly *Heaven and Earth* sets off sparks with the arrival of Tommy Lee Jones, as the one American soldier who isn't out to exploit this woman. But Mr. Jones, whose Sgt. Steve Butler is a composite of several men the real Ms. Hayslip knew, has a tough row to hoe. Steve changes from unbelievably nice guy into violent, abusive husband in record time, even if these are among the film's most colorful and involving episodes." And *Variety* critic Todd McCarthy felt that

"Jones tries to hit some unusual notes by emphasizing the vulnerable aspects of a professional killer, but that part of the tortured vet never becomes fully dimensional." *Newsweek*'s David Ansen thought: "There's enough material here for a mini-series. Crunched into 2 1/4 hours of spasmodic narrative, Le Ly's extraordinary life is reduced to its lurid highlights. . . . Some of the parts are undeniably gripping: what gets lost are the characters themselves. Jones's now charming, now desperate, now cuckoo soldier barely makes sense. . . ."

Butler pursues a reluctant Le Ly (Hiep Thi Le) . . .
(photo: Roland Neveu)

. . . gets to meet her young sons . . .

. . . and helps evacuate them by chopper at the city's downfall.

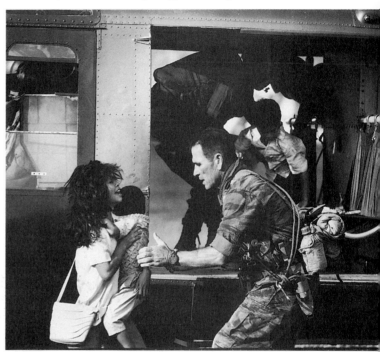

At home in America, growingly disheartened Butler and his mother (Debbie Reynolds) criticize Le Ly's Buddhist altar.

22

THE CLIENT

WARNER BROS., 1994

CAST

Susan Sarandon (*Reggie Love*), Tommy Lee Jones (*Roy Foltrigg*), Mary-Louise Parker (*Dianne Sway*), Anthony LaPaglia (*Barry Muldano*), J. T. Walsh (*Jason McThune*), Anthony Edwards (*Clint Von Hooser*), Brad Renfro (*Mark Sway*), Ossie Davis (*Judge Harry Roosevelt*), David Speck (*Ricky Sway*), Will Patton (*Sergeant Hardy*), Bradley Whitford (*Thomas Fink*), Anthony Heald (*Larry Truman*), Kim Coates (*Paul Gronke*), Kimberly Scott (*Doreen*), William H. Macy (*Dr. Greenway*), Micole Mercurio (*Momma Love*), William Sanderson (*Wally Boxx*), Walter Olkewicz (*Roney*), Amy Hathaway (*Nurse Karen*), Jo Harvey Allen (*Claudette*), Ron Dean (*Johnny Sulaki*), William Richert (*Harry Bond*), Will Zahn (*Call Beale*), Mark Cabus (*Det. Ed Nassar*), Dan Castellanetta (*Slick Moehler*), John Diehl (*Jack Nance*), and Tom Kacy, Ashton Tiller, Ruby Wilson, Andy Stahl, Ronnie Landry, Jeffry Ford, Macon McCalman, Michael Detroit, John Fink, Minnye Gore, Robert Hatchett, Connie Fluglance.

CREDITS

An Arnon Milchan production in association with Regency Enterprises and Alcor Films. *Producers,* Arnon Milchan and Steven Reuther; *coproducer,* Mary McLaglen; *director,* Joel Schumacher; *screenplay,* Akiva Goldman and Robert Getchell, *from the novel by* John Grisham; *cinematographer,* Tony Pierce-Roberts; *production designer,* Bruno Rubeo; *music,* Howard Shore; *editor,* Robert Brown. Technicolor and Panavision; *running time,* 120 minutes.

Two young brothers accidentally witness the suicide of a large bearded man, who turns out to be a mob lawyer, in the Tennessee woods after hearing his secret about the whereabouts of a murdered U.S. senator, and the chase is on in this adaptation of John Grisham's bestseller (the third to be filmed in a little over a year). The mob, in the person of psychotic Anthony LaPaglia, wants to shut them up and clean up the botched "hit." The feds, in the person of tenacious Tommy Lee Jones as a politically ambitious U.S. prosecutor, want the kids "in court and on the stand" to find out what they know. The older of the two brothers, an eleven-year-old played with verve by newcomer Brad Renfro, turns out to be remarkably resourceful in dodging the bad guys and the law while concerned over his younger sibling, who has lapsed into a psychosomatic coma and is hospitalized, and his single, trailer-park mom, who frets over both of them.

Entering the scene in a white stretch limo is dapper Jones as "Reverend" Roy Foltrigg, U.S. district attorney from New Orleans, flanked by, and barking orders to, a team of his own assistants and federal agents. "We gotta get our hands on that kid before the mob does," he orders. "I want that kid in court and on the stand mañana. Hear what I'm saying!" And in Jones's way of drawling, it is rapid-fire, a declarative sentence, not a question. Mark

THE CLIENT (1994): As scripture-quoting "Reverend" Roy Foltrigg, relentless federal prosecutor whose vocabulary does not include the word "losing"

Sway, the terrified boy on the run, however, decides he really could use some help—someone he can more or less trust who won't press him for too many answers that he's not ready to give, and he comes across one R. Love, attorney. R. Love turns out to be Reggie Love, a resilient divorcée played by Susan Sarandon (top-billed in an Oscar-nominated performance). She might have limited experience, but there's a personal commitment that young Mark instantly sees. After all, she knows not only the names of Led Zeppelin but also the titles of the group's first four albums, although he is still wary and isn't yet ready to reveal too much. He just wants her to protect him from the police. With feisty Reggie now running interference for him with fierce Roy, who finds he

has been temporarily buffaloed and is none too happy about it, sullen, scared Mark can try to sort things out in his own mind. But scowling, self-assured Roy is not one to be deterred from his single-minded mission. "You play big league hardball, Ms. Love. Now we don't sway to threats," he warns her when she tries some gentle, then brass-knuckled, negotiations with him. She snaps back: "I'm not going to let you use the child to climb into the governor's chair."

With grandstanding Roy and his men dogging her and scummy, handy-with-a-knife Barry Muldano (LaPaglia) closing in and wanting to make dogmeat of Mark before he can yap, Reggie and her young client ultimately have a meeting of the minds as the film's pace quickens.

Federal prosecutor Roy Foltrigg with feisty attorney Reggie Love and FBI agent Wally Boxx (William Sanderson, *left*) (photo: Demmie Todd)

Foltrigg dons a smiling façade as he prepares to parry with Reggie Love (Susan Sarandon) with the friendly warning "Miss a step and I'll eat you alive."

Ultimately, Mark is convinced to sit down with the feds for a chat, and after Roy sweet-talks the kid, he finds that Reggie has had her client wired with a recording device.

Eventually, Roy is able to get Mark on the stand before imperious Judge Harry Roosevelt (Ossie Davis) and tries to get him to tell what he knows, but what the boy knows is courtroom procedure from television, and he befuddles Scripture-quoting Roy Foltrigg et al. by inquiring about "taking the Fifth." Despite edgy Muldano and his thugs boldly stalking the halls of the courthouse and the hospital where Mark's younger brother is being treated, Mark and Reggie, now both in dire jeopardy, manage to flee the scene and hide out at her mom's secluded place in the sticks.

The plot turns somewhat sappy when Mark and Reggie become amateur sleuths, track down the grave of the dead senator, and come face-to-face with sinister Muldano and the boys. Grit and gumption are on the side of lawyer and client as they trip up the bad guys and break the case for Roy and the FBI. Putting on his best face, Roy negotiates with Reggie and fulfills a promise to place Mark, his brother, and their mom into the Federal Witness Protection Program. (To Mark it sadly means that he'll never again see his lawyer and partner in adventure.) He then turns his appreciative attention ever so briefly toward Reggie. One critic observed that Roy might even have had a thing for Reggie, finding in her a worthy adversary, if he already hadn't been in love with Roy.

Janet Maslin, in the *New York Times*, called Jones "just irresistible" and found that "his coiled-cobra gaze and that smart delivery remain in perfect form. Happily barking orders at his subordinates . . . preening for the television cameras, oozing Louisiana charm down to the tiniest y'all, Mr. Jones rivets attention." And in *New York* magazine, critic David Denby wrote: "As in *The Fugitive*, Tommy Lee Jones radiates energy and will and appears to be enjoying himself immensely. He gives Foltrigg his legendary quickness, his alertness and speed. Expensively dressed, moving through the world like a svelte express train, his Foltrigg is a rascally Southern showman who uses biblical quotations to drive home a point. But up close, he's quiet and deadly. When he threatens Reggie, there's an almost sexual intimacy in his voice."

Susan Sarandon's Academy Award nomination as

With straight-faced colleagues William Sanderson (*left*) and Bradley Whitford

Best Actress for the film gave Tommy Lee Jones a rather unique distinction in 1994—playing opposite two leading ladies who were Oscar contenders, the other Jessica Lange (the winner) in *Blue Sky*. Unfortunately, his own remarkable performance that year in another controver-sial film, *Cobb*, failed to garner him a nomination. During the 1995–96 TV season, *The Client* became a CBS series, with JoBeth Williams in the Sarandon role and John Heard in the one originated by Jones.

The attorney (Susan Sarandon), the prosecutor (Tommy Lee Jones), and the witness (Brad Renfro) (photo: Demmie Todd)

23

BLOWN AWAY

METRO-GOLDWYN-MAYER, 1994

CAST

Jeff Bridges (*Jimmy Dove*), Tommy Lee Jones (*Ryan Gaerity*), Suzy Amis (*Kate*), Lloyd Bridges (*Max O'Bannon*), Forest Whitaker (*Anthony Franklin*), Stephi Lineburg (*Lizzy*), John Finn (*Captain Roarke*), Caitlin Clarke (*Rita*), Chris De Omi (*Cortez*), Loyd Catlett (*Bama*), Ruben Santiago-Hudson (*Blanket*), Lucinda Weist (*Nancy*), Brendan Burns (*Kevin*), Patricia A. Heine (*Connie*), and John McLaglen, Ken Kerman, David Hodges, Robert "Bobby Z" Zajonc, Alan Purwin, David Howell, Dee Nelson, Judd Daniel King, Chris O'Neil, Whitney Cline, Michael Macklin, Sara Edwards, Evelyn Lee-Jones, Mark Berry, Faleena Hopkins.

CREDITS

A Trilogy Entertainment Group production. *Executive producer,* Lloyd Segan; *producers,* John Watson, Richard Lewis, and Pen Densham; *coproducer,* Dean O'Brien; *director,* Stephen Hopkins; *screenplay,* Joe Batteer and John Rice, *from a story by* Rice, Batteer, and M. Jay Roach; *cinematographer,* Peter Levy; *production designer,* John Graysmark; *music,* Alan Silvestri; *editor,* Timothy Wellburn. Deluxe color and Panavision; *running time,* 121 minutes.

Tommy Lee Jones plays a maniacal bomb-making IRA terrorist out to settle scores with a onetime protégé now working on the bomb squad with the Boston police in this muddled, very noisy thriller that had to compete at the box office in the summer of 1994 with the likes of *The Lion King,* Schwarzenegger's *True Lies,* and the megahit *Forrest Gump,* as well as his (Jones's) own film *The Client,* which premiered only weeks after this screen venture and possibly confused moviegoers because it bore the same title as the Corey Haim/Corey Feldman flick of several months earlier! It was no contest.

As *Blown Away* opens, Jones, as seething Ryan Gaerity, is seen wordlessly and dedicatedly assembling a bomb in his Northern Ireland prison cell. With rage consuming him, he recalls that a mate named Liam McGiveney twenty years earlier had bungled an Irish terrorist bombing he (Gaerity) had masterminded, causing the death of Gaerity's sister. Liam, now known as Jimmy Dove, has reestablished himself in America, and Gaerity ("He can make a bomb out of Bisquick!" one character notes), bent on revenge, blasts his way out of prison and turns up eventually in Boston. (Interpol, of course, is on his trail but cannot seem to pin him down—one of the many incongruities of the plot, which suffers from moviemaking shorthand.) He soon tracks down Dove, begins systematically making mincemeat of the city's bomb-disposal squad, and stalks him, his new wife, Kate, who is a violinist with the Boston Symphony, and her young daughter, Lizzy. Dove has spent two decades living with the Belfast tragedy—Gaerity's sister had been his sweetheart—and has been trying to move from active

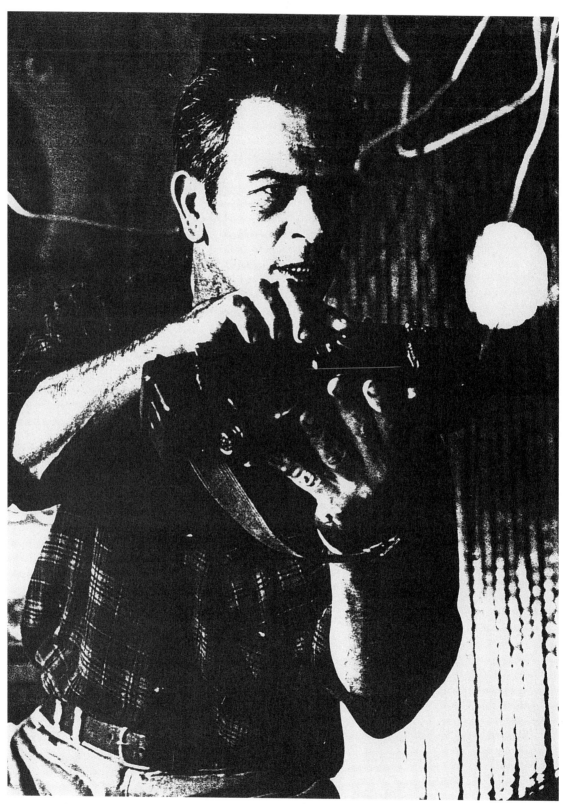

BLOWN AWAY (1994): Bomb-making fanatic Ryan Gaerity goes about his deadly business with a
vengeance (photo: Bruce Birmelin)

Showdown time when Jeff Bridges catches up with former IRA compatriot and mentor turned nemesis Tommy Lee Jones aboard a wreck moored at an abandoned dock in Boston harbor

duty on the squad, but Gaerity's diabolically crafted bombs keep turning up around Boston. Gaerity's cat-and-mouse tweaking eventually takes the life of several of Dove's colleagues and threatens to kill Dove's bumptious replacement on the squad, Anthony Franklin (Forest Whitaker), through a pair of ingeniously booby-trapped stereo headphones.

After discovering that Gaerity has broken into his house and possibly planted bombs in it (there are a tense few minutes during which assorted household appliances become suspect because of the director's ingenious camera angles), Dove races to hustle Kate and

Lizzy into hiding on Cape Cod and then gets a taunting call from his nemesis. "I'm not a destroyer; I'm a creator," Gaerity tells him. "I've come here to create a new country for you named chaos and a new government called anarchy." It isn't long before Gaerity turns up on the Cape in his guise as a beachcomber for a little friendly menace and a little musical U2, his favorite rock-group relaxation, while creating individualistic "toys" that Rube Goldberg would appreciate. He then puts in an insinuating appearance in an Irish bar in a working-class neighborhood of Boston and finds himself sharing a brew with Dove's grizzled old friend and mentor (Lloyd

Bridges in his Walter Brennan mode); in the next scene he has the elder Bridges strapped to a chair and an intricate bomb in his backyard. Dove finds the old man there but is powerless to prevent him from blowing up.

The spectacular set piece in a derelict tug tied up at a desolate Boston dock puts Dove face-to-face for the only time with Gaerity in the latter's bomb factory, which seems straight out of Frankenstein's lab, and in a confusing seven to ten minutes of fireworks and fireballs, the two antagonists go at one another with gusto. Ultimately, Gaerity gets himself incinerated as Franklin manages to rescue Dove. The film should end there, but it continues on to yet another climax set against a Boston Pops Fourth of July concert at the Esplanade, the famed band shell on the banks of the Charles River, where Kate is a member of the orchestra. As the music builds to the crescendo of the "1812 Overture," Dove races halfway across the city to save her, knowing that Gaerity has something evil in mind. Dove breathlessly arrives as the concertgoers are leaving, and Kate and her daughter drive off in their Jeep, which, it turns out, Gaerity has booby-trapped. And following a chase through the streets of Boston (à la *Speed*), Dove, who has somehow gotten aboard the speeding vehicle, miraculously manages to dismantle Gaerity's handiwork and save the day.

Since Jones is alone in nearly all of his scenes (he in-

Tommy Lee Jones discusses a scene with director Stephen Hopkins on the Boston location set.
(photo: Bruce Birmelin)

teracts with others in the cast at three isolated times), the Irish-brogued actor is seen maniacally tinkering, madly mumbling to himself, humming his favorite tunes, prancing around and keeping creative, especially in a drunken bomb-making sequence, in what is best characterized as a one-man madman performance. Most critics felt that the sometimes overwrought *Blown Away* fizzled and were distressed that both Jeff Bridges and Tommy Lee Jones were wasted in half-baked characterizations. "The script underuses Mr. Jones," critic Caryn James wrote in the *New York Times*, "and the supposed cat-and-mouse chase between the men degenerates into a series of awkward speeches. . . . No film with this cast could be a total waste, but [it] is surely one of the summer's major disappointments."

In Britain's *Monthly Film Bulletin* there was this observation: "Tommy Lee Jones as a demonic terrorist takes a while to warm to the job at hand. . . . But when he warms, he really warms. Not as natural as, say, Dennis Hopper might have been. Jones nonetheless attains two or three moments of true greatness here." And Jack Kroll noted in *Newsweek:* "Oscar-winner Jones is a master wacko and Bridges gives texture to a guy who has some bombs in his own belfry. This flick isn't dynamite, but it's no bomb."

24

NATURAL BORN KILLERS

WARNER BROS., 1994

CAST

Woody Harrelson (*Mickey Knox*), Juliette Lewis (*Mallory Knox*), Robert Downey Jr. (*Wayne Gale*), Tommy Lee Jones (*Warden Dwight McClusky*), Tom Sizemore (*Jack Scagnetti*), Rodney Dangerfield (*Mallory's dad*), Edie McClurg (*Mallory's mom*), Russell Means (*Old Indian*), Balthazar Getty (*Gas station attendant*), Joe Grifasi (*Duncan Homolka*), O-Lan Jones (*Mabel*), Dale Dye (*Dale Wrigley*), Ed White (*Pinball cowboy*), Richard Lineback (*Sonny*), Lanny Flaherty (*Earl*), Sean Stone (*Kevin*), Eddy "Boogie" Conna (*Gerald Nash*), Evan Handler (*David*), Kirk Baltz (*Roger*), Maria Pitillo (*Deborah*), Pruitt Taylor Vince (*Kavanaugh*), Sally Jackson (*Mickey's mom*), Phil Nelson (*Mickey's dad*), Brian Barker (*Young Mickey*), Corinna Laszlo (*Emily*), Red West (*Cowboy sheriff*), and Jerry Gardner, Jack Caffrey, Leon Skyhorse Thomas, Corey Everson, Terrylene, Josh Richman, Matthew Faber, Jamie Harrold, Jake Beecham, Jared Harris, Katherine McQueen, Natalie Karp, Salvator Xuereb, Emmanuel Xuereb, Gerry Runnels, Jeremiah Bitsui, Lorraine Ferris, Glen Chin, Everett Quinton, Marshall Bell, Bob Swan, Louis Lombardi.

CREDITS

An Ixtlan/New Regency production in association with Regency Enterprises, Alcor Films, and J. D. Productions. *Executive producers,* Arnon Milchan and Thom Mount; *producers,* Jane Hamsher, Don Murphy, and Clayton Townsend; *coproducer,* Rand Vossler; *director,* Oliver Stone; *screenplay,* David Veloz, Richard Rutowski, and Stone, *from a story by* Quentin Tarantino; *cinematographer,* Robert Richardson; *production designer,* Victor Kempster; *visual effects,* Pacific Data Images; *animation sequences,* Colossal Pictures; *editors,* Hank Corwin and Brian Berdan. Technicolor; *running time,* 119 minutes.

Controversy swirled around this lurid, extremely graphic, and quite savage satire on the American public's obsession with grotesque violence and the media's vulgar, pop-culture, trash-headline mayhem mania. Oliver Stone's most audacious and most highly stylized work to date, based on an original story by Quentin Tarantino and mixing off-kilter photography, cinema verité, animation, black-and-white inserts, dead animals, TV and movie clips, assorted psychedelics, and an incessant rock music track, found itself with either huzzahs or honest hatred from critics and public alike. There seemed to be no middle ground. It also later found itself (after long being out of the multiplexes and in the video stores) in the center of a political wrangle with Sen. Bob Dole's 1995 indictment of the movie industry and, in his view and that of conservative Republicans, its glorification of violence with bang-bang, kill-kill, shoot-'em-up

NATURAL BORN KILLERS (1994): Adopting his best glower as the sartorially splendid
Dwight McCluskey (photo: Sidney Baldwin)

Tom Sizemore as Det. Jack Scagnetti gets an earful from Tommy Lee Jones as Warden Dwight McCluskey over how to share the glare of the national media. (photo: Sidney Baldwin)

action films as entertainment at the expense of family values.

Natural Born Killers was actually a very bloody two-act acid trip dealing with an amoral killer and his teenage honey who go on a three-week midwestern killing spree in the sixties and gun down fifty-two people for kicks—and publicity (shades of the real-life Charlie Starkweather–Carol Fugate cross-country carnage of the fifties, as recounted in Terrence Malick's 1973 cult film *Badlands*). The first half focuses on a bad dude named Mickey Knox (Woody Harrelson), an escaped convict, who sets his sights on trashy, underage chick Mallory (Juliette Lewis) and rescues her from her lecherous dad (Rodney Dangerfield). They begin the murder rampage by shooting her folks and then leave a trail of blood through New Mexico, usually with one survivor to tell the tale. Thrill-crazy Mickey and Mallory, all lust, become instant media celebrities and find themselves spotlighted on a TV show called *American Maniacs*, hosted by Wayne Gale (Robert Downey Jr., in a devastating takeoff on Robin Leach), a grating, ratings-obsessed Australian who connives to trail along with the murderous pair to capture the moments on camera. He's bent on grabbing the biggest audience ever by interviewing Mickey and Mallory live opposite the Super Bowl.

Ultimately, the natural born killers are nabbed and sent to prison, and in the film's second half, the battle of

publicity and public opinion is waged. Enter good old boy and slightly off the wall Warden Dwight McClusky (Tommy Lee Jones, with a pencil mustache, a sadistic chuckle, and a crazed glint in his eye), who giddily plans to assassinate Mickey and Mallory and grab the publicity spotlight, and leering, unhinged cop Jack Scagnetti (Tom Sizemore), who hopes to write a bestseller about the Romeo and Juliet killers. McClusky brags to Scagnetti about "offing" the two celebrity prisoners: "If I don't, we'll be excoriated in the press. If I do, it'll still be weeks before they clear us. Them'll be toast before that ever happens."

Mickey throws everything awry in a volcanic riot that he instigates during one of Wayne Gale's tapings. Much of the riot sequence, including a scene in which Warden McClusky is decapitated and his head is impaled on a stick to the delight of the inmates, was deleted from the final print of the film, but Oliver Stone hoped to have it restored in his "director's cut" for the 1996 video and laser-disc release, along with other debaucheries.

With the riot in full fury, the reunited couple escape, with Gale in tow (and madly taping). All ends bloodily—in the Oliver Stone emblematic tradition. Gale is executed before his own camera, and Mickey and Mallory go off to live as a nuclear family in a trailer home. And

just before the final credits roll, there is a montage of tabloid television's celebrity killers and suspects—from O. J. Simpson and Erik and Lyle Menendez to Tonya Harding and Lorena Bobbitt.

The rather brief role of the maniacally delusional, somewhat dense, almost cartoonish McClusky allowed Tommy Lee Jones (in his third Oliver Stone movie) one of his most over the top performances, on a par with his earlier one in Andrew Davis's *Under Siege* and his subsequent one in Joel Schumacher's *Batman Forever.* (Critic Michael Medved observed in the *New York Post:* "[He] not only chews the scenery but literally gets to climb the walls.") Musing on his role in a *Film Comment* cover story, Jones said: "You pick things that you find *ridiculous,* worthy of satire. So we tried to think up as many stupid things as we possibly could. I've always thought those little pencil-thin mustaches were really stupid. Huge Carl Perkins sideburns. They said, 'What do you want your hair to look like?' I said, 'I think it ought to look like a '57 Studebaker.' . . . The idea was that he's an elegant man, in his own mind. The world revolves around him, so it's important to be quite beautiful, elegant. So these are signs of elegance. We picked the ugliest gold rings we could figure. It was all about how wrong a person can be." Buffs might note a sly Jones homage to one

In his three-piece suit complete with boutonniere, perfect attire for a warden at a high-risk prison, McCluskey throws his weight around. (photo: Sidney Baldwin)

143

of his first Hollywood roles: The swinging on the cell bars, here as warden, mirrors what he did as a convict two decades before in *Jackson County Jail.*

"Jones is broader than he's ever been as the sweaty lip-smacking warden none too good at his job," *Variety* critic Todd McCarthy wrote. "Film's style may be akin to a shotgun blast, but it still manages to hit the bull's eye." Jami Bernard noted in the New York *Daily News:* "Armed with superb acting and an outrageous idea—a serial killing couple who become media darlings—Oliver Stone batters you over the head with *Natural Born Killers,* a satire on our trash-media culture that would have prof-

ited from a lighter hand. . . . Tommy Lee Jones turns loose yet another junkyard-dog authoritative figure, this time as a self-impressed warden." In *Time,* Richard Corliss wrote: "*Natural Born Killers* plunders every trick of avant-garde and mainstream media—morphing, back projection, slow motion, animation, and pixilations on five kinds of film stock—and for two delicious hours, pushes them in your face like a Cagney grapefruit." Of Jones, he observed: "As the smarmy prison warden [he] does a wonderfully demented variation on his Texarkana-tough-guy-in-authority shtick."

McCluskey goes wacko as the Batongaville Prison riot erupts. (photo: Sidney Baldwin)

25

BLUE SKY

ORION PICTURES, 1994 (FILMED 1991)

CAST

Jessica Lange (*Carly Marshall*), Tommy Lee Jones (*Hank Marshall*), Powers Boothe (*Vince Johnson*), Carrie Snodgress (*Vera Johnson*), Amy Locane (*Alex Marshall*), Chris O'Donnell (*Glenn Johnson*), Mitchell Ryan (*Ray Stevens*), Dale Dye (*Col. Mike Anwalt*), Tim Scott (*Ned Owens*), Annie Ross (*Lydia*), Anna Kemp (*Becky Marshall*), Michael McClendon (*Lt. Col. Bob Jennings*), Merlin Marston (*Lt. Col. George Land*), Dion Anderson (*General Derrick*), Richard Jones (*Jimmy*), Gary Bullock (*Dr. Vankay*), Angela Paton (*Dottie Owens*), and Anthony Rene Jones, Jay H. Seidl, David Bradford, Matt Battaglia, Rene Rokk, Fred Scasso, Victor Iemolo, Bronson Page, Raphael Rey Gomez, Samy G. Bauso, John J. Fedak, Harriet Courtney Sumner, Shannon Laramore, Ray Sergeant, Yvette Smedley, Phyllis Timbes, Libby Whittemore, Clarinda Ross, Donna Biscoe, Billy Lawson, Joseph Wilkins, Carl C. Morgan III, Art Wheeler, Sharlene Ross, David Lee Lane, Ed Lee Corbin, Babs George.

CREDITS

Producer, Robert H. Solo; *coproducer,* Lynn Arost; *director,* Tony Richardson; *screenplay,* Rama Laurie Stagner, Arlene Sarner, and Jerry Leichtling, *from a story by* Stagner; *cinematography,* Steve Yaconelli; *production design,* Timian Alsaker; *music,* Jack Nitzsche; *editor,* Robert K. Lambert. CFI color; *running time,* 101 minutes.

A stunning romantic drama, *Blue Sky* (the title refers to a top-secret military operation dealing with A-bomb tests in the American West in the sixties) was an anomaly in films. Produced in 1991 by British director Tony Richardson, it sat on the shelf for several years while the studio that financed it found itself in Chapter 11—despite a string of critically acclaimed box-office hits like back-to-back Oscar winners *Dances With Wolves* and *The Silence of the Lambs.* Meanwhile, Richardson died of AIDS shortly after its completion, and stars Jessica Lange and Tommy Lee Jones moved on to other stage and screen projects. Lange went to Broadway and got good notices in *A Streetcar Named Desire,* while Jones, in fact, made four more films before *Blue Sky* was belatedly released.

Jones and Lange (who had earlier starred together in a television version of *Cat on a Hot Tin Roof*) and their two daughters make up a military family. He's an army scientist involved with America's nuclear program, and she's a bored sexpot of a wife with a tendency toward manic depression. The film opens with a remarkable shot of Lange, as Carly Marshall, sunbathing topless on a beach and Jones, as Hank Marshall, in an army helicopter bursting with pride as he shows off his wife to the pilot who is buzzing her. Carly's sexy antics on the beach and around the military base soon gets her husband, a career officer, in hot water. During a dressing-down by his superior, Hank tells him in a precise, clipped, stiff-

BLUE SKY (1994): Jones and Jessica Lange as Hank and Carly Marshall share a happy moment in their combustible marriage. (photo: Cliff Lipson)

backed military manner, "My job is to evaluate radiation hazards to United States Army personnel. My wife is not enlisted in the army. Why doesn't the colonel concern himself with men who are rather than the mammaries of women who are not." Hank, Carly, and daughters Alex and Becky soon find themselves transferred from Hawaii to a new post in Alabama. There Carly, who fantasizes about a Hollywood career (she dresses initially as Bardot, moves on to Monroe, and ends up in the Elizabeth Taylor mode), views their shabby new quarters and goes into a funk before beginning to sashay around the base tantalizingly.

She soon attracts the attention of Vince Johnson (Powers Boothe), the womanizing commanding officer (CO) who flaunts his predilection in the face of his wife, Vera (Carrie Snodgress). Incredibly patient, stoic Hank keeps his peace, though aware of what's going down, coping with domestic chores until Carly rallies from her funk. The lecherous CO, whose teenage son Glenn (Chris O'Donnell) has discovered the blossoming Alex Marshall, continues making a play for the restless, live-wire Carly. He gets Hank out of the way by sending him

off to the Blue Sky project in Nevada, where underground nuclear tests are under way. There Hank learns that two cowboys who had inadvertently wandered into the test range have become victims of nuclear fallout, but his efforts to make things safer fall on deaf ears. Back in Alabama, Carly and Vince are caught in flagrante delicto by her daughter and his son, and news spreads around the base. She quickly becomes snubbed by the other officers' wives.

Alex urges her mother to call Hank and confess her betrayal, and when he returns to his base from Nevada, he has a confrontation with his CO both about Carly and about the Blue Sky project. Carly is then persuaded by the army to have Hank committed to a psychiatric hospital in order to shut him up after he threatens to go public about the nuclear test, and she soon finds that he has been heavily drugged. Seeing his spirit broken, she decides that to secure his release she must take matters into her own hands—by exposing the Blue Sky project to media attention by going to the Nevada test site, riding to the center on horseback, getting arrested, and drawing the interest of reporters.

Carly is comforted by Hank when they confront the aftermath of her unpredictable behavior: a new, less glamorous military assignment. (photo: Cliff Lipson)

147

The Marshalls in more joyous times (photo: Cliff Lipson)

Director Tony Richardson shooting his last film (photo: Cliff Lipson)

She then negotiates with the army to remain silent if Hank is released from the hospital and honorably discharged and Vince Johnson is relieved of his command. The united Marshall family then finds itself bound for Berkeley, California, where Hank can assume a faculty post and begin expounding on his antinuclear philosophy.

The *New York Times*'s Caryn James hailed *Blue Sky* as "among [Tony] Richardson's finest work . . . a magnificent period piece," and noted that "Mr. Jones's performance matches Ms. Lange's in strength and subtlety. Hank is a tough, controlled military man whose competence masks the strain of caring for his wife . . . a patient, frustrated man coming to the end of his rope. . . . The understated depths Mr. Jones reaches offers a reminder of his range after a series of over-the-top character roles in films like *The Client* and *Natural Born Killers*." In the *New York Post*, critic Thelma Adams called the characters played by the two leads "the F. Scott and Zelda Fitzgerald of the military set" and felt that "Jones, the comforting calm of his voice the iron bar the family clings to, demonstrates a range and control only hinted at in his three [most recent] movies. [His] power here is in the quiet moments, rather than the over-the-top rages and exhibitionistic bits that showcase Lange."

In *Variety* there was this opinion by reviewer Todd McCarthy: "Two fine actors give among the best performances of their careers in *Blue Sky*. . . . While Lange has the showy role, with almost unlimited opportunities to emote and strut her stuff, which she does magnificently and with total abandon, Jones must let his characterization take shape more gradually. But his Hank ultimately emerges as fully three-dimensional, as does his wife, with the actor demonstrating terrific control and nuance on a tight rein." And Britain's *Sight and Sound* said, "Tommy Lee Jones, in the more subtle but possibly more challenging role of Hank, reaffirms what a fine actor he is. By the most delicate of gestures and expressions he conveys both the rigidity and the sexual obsessiveness so crucial to the character and so unexplained and avoided by the dialogue."

Jessica Lange won the Academy Award as Best Actress for her performance in *Blue Sky* as Carly Marshall. Hers was the single nomination given to the film, although many critics felt that Tommy Lee Jones had given the finest performance of his career to date.

26

COBB

WARNER BROS., 1994

CAST

Tommy Lee Jones (*Ty Cobb*), Robert Wuhl (*Al Stump*), Lolita Davidovich (*Ramona*), Lou Myers (*Willie*), Stephen Mendillo (*Mickey Cochrane*), Eloy Casados (*Louis Prima*), William Utay (*Jameson*), J. Kenneth Campbell (*Prof. William Henschel Cobb*), Tommy Bush (*Rogers Hornsby*), Ned Bellamy (*Ray*), Scott Burkholder (*Jimmy*), Allan Malamud (*Mud*), Rhoda Griffis (*Ty's mother*), Tyler Logan Cobb (*Young Ty*), Paula Rudy (*Keely Smith*), Ernie Harwell (*MC at Hall of Fame banquet*), Reid Cruickshanks (*Pie Traynor*), Stacy Keach Sr. (*Jimmy Foxx*), Janice Certain (*Cobb's daughter*), Tracy Keehn-Dashnaw (*Cobb's wife*), Roger Clemens (*Opposing pitcher*), and Bill Caplan, Jeff Fellenzer, Doug Kirkorian, Gavin Smith, Rev. Gary Morris, Jerry J. Gatlin, Harold Herthum, Jay Chevalier, George Rafferty, Jay Tibbs, Rodney Max, Gary D. Talbert, Fred Lewis, David Hodges, Joy Michiel, Artie Butler, Rath Shelton, Jim Shelton, Clive Rosengren, Jimmy Buffett, Don Hood, Brian Mulligan, Jerry Hauck.

CREDITS

A Regency Enterprises/Alcor Films production. *Executive producer*, Arnon Milchan; *producer*, David Lester; *writer-director*, Ron Shelton; *based on the book* Cobb: A Biography *by* Al Stump; *cinematographer*, Russell Boyd; *production designers*, Armin Ganz and Scott Ritenour; *music*, Elliot Goldenthal; *editors*, Paul Seydor and Kimberly Ray. Technicolor and Panavision; *running time*, 128 minutes.

Tyrus Raymond Cobb was a legend, generally considered the greatest hitter ever to play professional baseball, ferocious at bat and on the field from before World War I until his retirement in 1928. He was also by nearly all accounts the cruelest, most bigoted, mean-spirited, detestable son of a bitch on the diamond or off. Tommy Lee Jones's frightening portrayal of Cobb in the twilight of his years, as written by director Ron Shelton, was a one-man performance of epic proportion—actually it was a two-man story, sportswriter Al Stump (played by Robert Wuhl), Cobb's biographer, was the other. "The only thing that matters in this life is a man's accomplishments," Cobb demands of Stump, "and I must say, Al, in all humility—in *all* humility—I'm the greatest baseball player of all time; nobody even comes close to that!"

Cobb the movie, one critic pointed out, is not really about Cobb the man or even about baseball. It is rather about the symbiotic relationship that developed between the bombastic, dying Cobb and writer Stump. It opens with Stump arriving at the pistol-waving Cobb's snowbound Tahoe residence in 1960, ostensibly to collaborate on a book on the man once known as the Georgia Peach but secretly to write what he feels is Cobb's real story while concocting a whitewashed version. What greets him is a cantankerous, bourbon-swilling, impotent paranoid. Stump has laid himself open for an unending browbeating, a drinking and carousing spree through Reno, and a nonstop stream of verbal

COBB (1994): As egotistical, ever-angry Ty Cobb (photo: Sidney Baldwin)

151

abuse as septuagenarian Cobb's Boswellian whipping boy, being bellowed at (and bellowing back) during a cross-country drive from the Rockies to a testimonial dinner for Cobb in Cooperstown, New York. Along the way, Stump learns of some of Cobb's darkest personal secrets that sparked his brutal personality. Then it's on to Royston, Georgia, where Cobb was born. There Cobb's daughter refuses to speak with him. Also there Cobb discovers Stump's notes for a second book and flies into a rage, which ends with his coughing up blood, checking into a hospital, and dying. Stump decides to finish his book the way Cobb would have wanted it.

Jones sinks his teeth into the role and plays Cobb as, in the eyes of Richard Schickel in *Time*, "pure attack dog." Terrence Rafferty (*The New Yorker*) found that "the dying Cobb that [Ron] Shelton and Jones have put in the screen is a fascinating and appalling creature—a monster of mythic proportions, bellowing and thrashing and belching fire right to the end. He's a man who sees

movie acting of 1994 . . . we're clearly seeing an actor take a role to its limit." Wilmington continued: "There's a naked savagery, a fury and recklessness, in Jones's performance that you rarely see in movies about legendary historical figures. His eyes burn; his voice rakes the air. . . he catches the essence of Ty Cobb, his warrior heart. . . . If acting were scored like baseball, Tommy Lee Jones, like Ty Cobb in 1909, would take the triple crown."

Critic Dave Kehr wrote in the New York *Daily News* that "Jones plays Cobb with a flat-out intensity, relishing the ripe accent and extravagant gestures. There are few quiet moments to provide contrast or depth, and no scenes on the field to suggest why Cobb was such a great

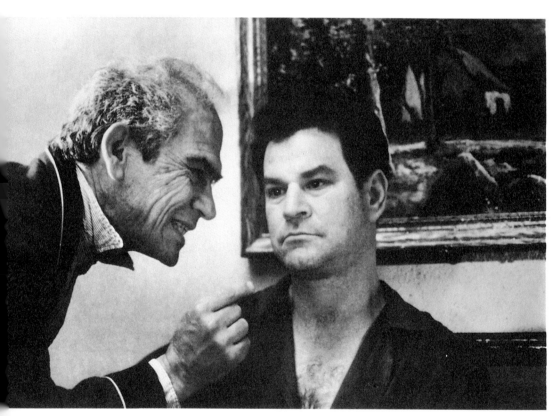

Tommy Lee's Cobb browbeats his rather stoic Bosworth, sportswriter Al Stump (Robert Wuhl). (photo: Sidney Baldwin)

no reason why he shouldn't get his way; he views other people primarily as impediments to the satisfaction of his desires."

Michael Wilmington (*Chicago Tribune*) thought that *Cobb* hit one out of the park, giving the film four stars, and he was beside himself with praise for Tommy Lee Jones, calling his portrayal of Cobb "the major American player." *Variety*'s Leonard Klady observed: "Jones plays Cobb on a Shakespearean scale, with obvious parallels between the Georgia Peach and King Lear." And in *People Weekly*, Ralph Novak decided: "Jones's acting doesn't need much broadening these days, but he fits his performance into Shelton's bombastic script; there's scarcely a hint of subtlety. He does, though, effectively suggest some of the anguish the great athlete must have felt as his panther's body deteriorated underneath him."

Entertainment Weekly's Owen Gleiberman was stunned: "Not since Bette Davis moldered and shrieked through *What Ever Happened to Baby Jane?* has an actor this talented been allowed to indulge in this much garish Southern gothic hysteria. . . . If anyone could dig into the demons that drove Ty Cobb, could tap the ugly truth and, at the same time, locate the warped humanity behind it, Jones, with his feral intelligence, his malignance and strength, would seem to be the one. . . . Cobb, however, is a jaw-dropping botch, a bilious and reductive attack on its own hero." Britain's *Sight and Sound* judged that perhaps the film should have been called "Citizen Cobb": "To its credit . . . this soft pastiche of *Citizen Kane* enhances the film's true colours which are surprisingly richer than those of the average biopic." The magazine's critic said of its star: "Having made a career out of playing good ol' boys with nasty streaks, Tommy Lee Jones nails the type down forever."

Following the revisionist autobiography *My Life in*

Lolita Davidovich, as a Reno hooker, makes an aging Cobb feel frisky. (photo: Sidney Baldwin)

Cobb threatens a casino patron in Reno while Al Stump and security people try to stop him. (photo: Sidney Baldwin)

Baseball, on which he collaborated with his "hero," Stump published the real story on which Ron Shelton, whose earlier baseball movie *Bull Durham* was much admired, based this film—which despite Jones's bravura performance and Wuhl's engaging one, unfortunately wasn't by moviegoers. "Although Mr. Jones gives the film the entertaining demon it needs," Janet Maslin (*New York Times*) wrote, "*Cobb* is finally nowhere near as tough as the man was himself."

To Cobb, imminent death is no reason for forsaking a good cigar. (photo: Sidney Baldwin)

27

BATMAN FOREVER

WARNER BROS., 1995

CAST

Val Kilmer (*Bruce Wayne/Batman*), Tommy Lee Jones (*Harvey "Two-Face" Dent*), Jim Carrey (*Edward Nygma/The Riddler*), Nicole Kidman (*Dr. Chase Meridian*), Chris O'Donnell (*Dick Grayson/Robin*), Michael Gough (*Alfred Pennyworth*), Pat Hingle (*Commissioner Gordon*), Drew Barrymore (*Sugar*), Debi Mazar (*Spice*), Ed Begley Jr. (*Fred Stickley*), Elizabeth Sanders (*Gossip Gerty*), René Auberjonois (*Dr. Burton*), Joe Grifasi (*Bank Guard*), Philip Moon and Jessica Tuck (*Newscasters*), Dennis Paladino (*Crime Boss Moroni*), Kimberly Scott (*Margaret*), Ramsey Ellis (*Young Bruce Wayne*), Michael Scranton (*Thomas Wayne*), Eileen Seeley (*Martha Wayne*), George Wallace (*Mayor*), and Michael Paul Chan, Jon Favreau, Greg Lauren, David U. Hodges, Jack Betts, Tim Jackson, Daniel Reichert, Glory Fioramonti, Larry A. Lee, Bruce Roberts, Don "The Dragon" Wilson, Gary Kasper, Andrea Fletcher, John Fink.

CREDIT

A Tim Burton production; *Executive producers*, Benjamin Melniker and Michael E. Uslan; *producers*, Tim Burton and Peter Macgregor-Scott; *director*, Joel Schumacher; *screenplay*, Lee Batchler, Janet Scott Batchler, and Akiva Goldsman, *from a story by* Lee Batchler and Janet Scott Batchler, *based upon characters created by* Bob Kane; *cinematographer*, Stephen Goldblatt; *production designer*, Barbara Ling; *art directors*, Chris Burian-Mohr, James Hegedus, and Joe Lucky; *special effects supervisor*, John Dykstra; *special makeup designed and created by* Rick Baker; *editor*, Dennis Virkler; *music*, Elliot Goldenthal. Technicolor and Panavision; *running time*, 121 minutes.

The third of Tim Burton's Batman movies (although here Burton functioned merely as coproducer) opened, if not to ecstatic critical acclaim, at least to the biggest set of box office grosses in film history—for a nonholiday weekend. And amid all the preopening hype, the massive merchandising campaign, and the plethora of Bat tchotchkes to fill Warners coffers, there was Tommy Lee Jones in an uncharacteristic (if not really comfortable) live-action cartoon role as schizophrenic Harvey "Two-Face" Dent.

As change-of-race Two-Face, a onetime Gotham City district attorney (played in the first Batman movie in 1989 by Billy Dee Williams) whose face was disfigured on the left side by acid and frozen in a permanent leer, Tommy Lee—if not Billy Dee—now dressed for the part, his body completely divided down the middle—the hair on the left side of his head flaming red and frizzed out, on the right, slicked back in black; his garb wild and crazy on the left, conservative on the right; his left side a riot of gaudy decadence, his right side sartorially splendid. He sported a babe on each arm—seductive Debi Mazar as Spice on the left, unexpectedly demure Drew Barrymore as Sugar on the right, and he sipped two martinis as the same time, one from each side of his mouth. Even his lair has two faces, being split down the middle, with one side out of *House and Gardens*, the other, which he straddles, a tribute to gauchery.

157

BATMAN FOREVER (1995): As Two-Face, schizophrenic criminal mastermind (photo: Ralph Nelson)

As a faux ringmaster he prepares to create havoc at a Gotham circus. (photo: Ralph Nelson)

Two-Face intimidates a guard (Joe Grifasi) at the Second Bank of Gotham into giving him a "loan"—a BIG one! (photo: Ralph Nelson)

Unfortunately, he had to compete for screen time and spectacular scenery to chew with another Batman villain, Riddler, played by the maniacal, rubber-faced Jim Carrey. Even in a Batman movie two outrageous villains, especially when they are playing in two disparate styles, is one too many. Jones, not being a natural comic actor, proved to be at a distinct, if garish, disadvantage, and as pointed out by *Variety* critic Brian Lowry, "Aside from a wild cackle [Jones] has little to do and lets his gruesome makeup do all the acting."

As in the two previous and decidedly darker Batman movies, in 1989 and 1992, the outrageous villains, the comic book–like production design, and the spectacular special effects manage to make the nominal hero rather dull and the plot secondary. In fact, in the third installment, much has changed—new leading man (square-jawed Val Kilmer in for square-jawed Michael Keaton), newly added Robin (unseen and unmentioned in the earlier films), new hard-bodied superhero costumes, new Batmobile, new bad guys, new femme fatale,

160

new director, new writers, new music composer. Actually, the only constants linking all three movies were the same studio and actors Michael Gough as Alfred, Bruce Wayne's discreet butler, and Pat Hingle as Gotham City's police commissioner.

In the third, spectacularly appointed, if rather darkly photographed and messily scripted, installment, raving, punning, coin-flipping Two-Face is out to avenge the acid bath he claims Batman gave him and turns out to be the one responsible for teenage circus acrobat Dick Grayson—Bruce Wayne's "ward," as has been established in comic-book lore—losing his family. With E. Nygma, overlooked, if rather weird employee, at Wayne Enterprises turned supercriminal posing as an urbane entrepreneur, Two-Face hatches a sinister scheme to uncover Batman's identity, intrudes with his gang on an elegant "do" being thrown by his preening colleague, the Riddler ("It's only an old-fashioned low-tech stickup," he commands the guests. "We're only interested in the basics—cash, jewelry, cellular telephones"), and ends up not only invading stately Wayne manor and destroying the Batcave below but also kidnapping beautiful criminal psychologist Chase Meridian, whose main pursuit is also Batman.

Two-Face, according to the Warner Bros. production notes, first appeared in *Detective Comics* number 66 in 1942, but DC Comics gave him a rest twelve years later. He was recalled to wreak more havoc in 1971. Tommy

With Riddler (Jim Carrey), fellow archvillain (photo: Ralph Nelson)

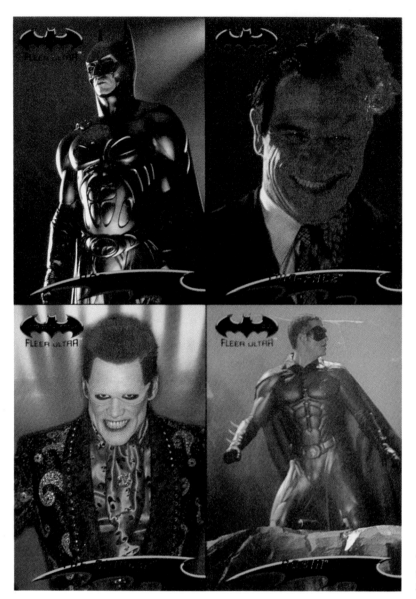

Tommy Lee Jones is a participant in the massive merchandising campaign for *Batman Forever*.

162

Getting his comeuppance in his showdown with the Caped Crusader (photo: Ralph Nelson)

Lee Jones is the first to portray the bizarre, scarred Two-Face as a live-action performer. "With *Batman Forever*, we're living in a world of comic books," Tommy Lee said. "Two-Face is a bifurcated character, Jekyll-and-Hyde simplified to the cartoon level." And he played the character even more outrageously than he did as gleefully batty Warden Dwight McCloskey in *Natural Born Killers* and baseball bastard Ty Cobb, in a number of scenes, in *Cobb* (the latter, of course, not meant to be an over-the-top crazy).

"Given that in *Batman Forever* the text is all about subtext, no real story emerges. Batman chases Two-Face, the Riddler chases Batman, Dr. Meridian chases Bruce Wayne, and so on. It's a lot of bat-and-mouse," Britain's *Sight and Sound* reported. "There's two of everything," critic Dave Kehr pointed out in his *New York Daily News* review. "Two main villains, both of whom have two identities (Jones' Harvey is a one-man Jekyll and Hyde rou-

tine, combining good and bad sides in one figure) and two main heroes." In *Entertainment Weekly*, Owen Gleiberman noted that "[Jones's] Two-Face is a rip-snorting hooligan whose face—or at least half of it—has been deformed by acid in a purplish mash of vein and sinew (it looks like an exploding eggplant). . . . Unfortunately, the role doesn't give Jones much to do besides scowl under his ugly makeup."

Hal Hinson (*Washington Post*) felt that "as Two-Face . . . Jones gives a reprise of his no-holds-barred performance in Cobb (though with far less gratifying results)." And in *New York Newsday*, Jack Mathews noted that "the performances of Jim Carrey and Tommy Lee Jones, [are] both so over-the-top they can give you a headache. . . . Jones, however, is not a natural clown, and it's painful to watch him trying to hold the screen with Carrey. Two-Face is a sight gag [but] not enough of a sight gag to warrant all the jokey riffs done on it, and it leaves Jones with nothing to do but wail about what a cruel, cruel world it is. For actors and villains." Jack Knoll's take in *Newsweek* on *Batman Forever:* "It's Batman's evil adversaries that are crucial, and here the movie badly lets down Tommy Lee Jones as Two-Face, the acid-scarred archfiend. Unlike Jack Nicholson's Joker in the first *Batman*, Jones has little to do but cackle insanely and endlessly flip a coin, his method for determining his victim's fate. Too much cackle-and-flip gets awfully wearing."

Two-Face and Riddler are at odds on how to destroy the Dynamic Duo. (photo: Ralph Nelson)

28

VOLCANO

TWENTIETH CENTURY–FOX, 1997

CAST

Tommy Lee Jones (*Mike Roark*), Anne Heche (*Dr. Amy Barnes*), Gaby Hoffman (*Kelly Roark*), Don Cheadle (*Emmit Reese*), Jacqueline Kim (*Dr. Jaye Calder*), Keith David (*Lt. Ed Fox*), John Corbett (*Norman Calder*), Michael Rospoli (*Gator Harris*), John Carroll Lynch (*Stan Olber*), Marcello Thedford (*Kevin*), Laurie Lathem (*Rachel*), Bert Remsen (*Fire Chief*), Bo Eason (*Bud McVie*), James G. MacDonald (*Terry Jasper*), Dayton Callie (*Roger Lapher*), Michael Cutt (*Armstrong*), Kevin Bourland (*Bob Davis*), Lou Myers (*Pastor Lake*), Susie Essman (*Anita*), Mickey Cottrell (*Councilman Gates*), and Valente Rodriguez, Sheila Howard, Gerry Black, Gareth Williams, Juan Gabriel Reynoso, Angela Albarez, Richard Penn, Jennifer Bill, M. Darnell Suttles, Ken Kerman, Sal Rendino, Michael Manuel, Jared Thorne, Taylor Thorne, Richard Schiff, Brad Parker, Pete Kasper, Brian Markinson, Robert Wisdom, Wayne Grace, Mother Love.

CREDITS

Executive producer, Lauren Shuler Donner; *producers*, Neil H. Moritz and Andrew Z. Davis; *coproducers*, Michael Fottrell and Stokely Chaffin; *director*, Mick Jackson; *screenplay*, Jerome Armstrong and Billy Ray; *story*, Armstrong and Moritz; *cinematographer*, Theo van de Sande; *production designer*, Jackson DeGovia; *music*, Alan Silvestri; *editors*, Michael Tronick and Don Brochu; *visual effects supervisor*, Mat Beck. Deluxe color; *running time*, 104 minutues.

As L.A.'s chief of the Office of Emergency Management, and a transplanted flood fighter, tough Tommy Lee Jones—billed alone above the title—had his chance to carry a $100 million big-budget movie and fight a local calamity. Unfortunately, the outsized special effects reduced the actual plot to about fifteen minutes. The film came on the heels of another volcano flick, *Dante's Peak*, a box-office loser released not long before *Volcano* (actually they had been scheduled to open almost simultaneously), and a made-for-television movie called *Volcano: Fire on the Mountain.*

Volcano opened to lots of hype with the catchphrase, "The Coast Is Toast!," which is destined to rank among the immortal ad lines in cinema history—right up there, probably, with "Garbo Speaks!," "Gable's Back and Garson's Got Him," "Love Means Never Having to Say You're Sorry," and "Just When You Thought It Was Safe to Go Back Into the Water." The film premiered really big—at number one the opening weekend—but unfortunately languished at the box office after that. Speculative reasons: audiences found there was no volcano in the film—just an oozing and exploding La Brea Tar Pits in the middle of Los Angeles that threatened to decimate the town; nothing for normally dynamic Tommy Lee Jones and cast to do but react to the cataclysm and stay a step or two ahead of the insidiously flowing lava; and most devastating of all—considering this was a mass destruction flick—the public "coming out" of costar Anne

Heche the very day the picture opened and stealing all the publicity.

Basically, the film finds its macho star at ground zero when the La Brea Tar Pits erupt and lava begins flowing in the streets. Manhole covers are blown into the sky, subway trains are engulfed in fireballs, fire trucks are melting on every corner, miniature sets are ablaze from "lava bombs" flying through the air—all that good stuff that's at the core of disaster flicks. There are also the nearly obligatory elements with which the take-charge hero (here a divorced workaholic) must contend: a whining quarrelsome teenage daughter with whom to reestablish a fatherly bond; a spiky blond seismologist/geologist, prone to exclaiming "Oh, God!" who shrilly tells her male companion the facts of the situation and then becomes his copartner in distress; a fast-talking sidekick back at the office shouting over the phone and taking verbal abuse from his superior; a compassionate female doctor to take care of matters back at the ER; and even a puppy to upstage actors and effects.

Under the headline: "Lava in La-La Land: Tommy Lee Jones to the Rescue," Roger Ebert smirked in his syndicated review that, "This is a surprisingly cheesy disaster epic...Dante's Peak had better special effects, a more entertaining story and a real mountain. Volcano is an absolutely standard, assembly-line undertaking." Ebert admitted that "Jones [is] professional as always even in this flimsy story...[He] is a fine actor and does what he can." Newsweek's David Ansen, who gave Volcano one of its few raves, found that "Jones and Heche have to create their characters on the run, and skimpy as these roles are, they give them urgency and a plausible aura of intelligence." Ansen concluded that, "Volcano busily and cheerfully hysterical, always has some new fish to fry, new truck to melt, new skyscraper to tumble, or new manhole to pop with a radiant gusher of movie magma."

VOLCANO: Jones makes a run for it with daughter Gaby Hoffman as L.A. begins erupting. (photo: Lorey Sebastian)

VOLCANO: The cataclysmic destruction of the City of Angels (it ain't just corn flakes) momentarily engulfs Tommy Lee Jones and Anne Heche. (photo: Lorey Sebastian)

VOLCANO: Jones and Heche hangin' in there as the coast turns to toast. (photo: Lorey Sebastian)

29

MEN IN BLACK

AMBLIN ENTERTAINMENT/COLUMBIA PICTURES, 1997

CAST

Tommy Lee Jones (*K*), Will Smith (*J*), Linda Fiorentino (*Laurel*), Vincent D'Onofrio (*Edgar*), Rip Torn (*Zed*), Tony Shalhoub (*Jeebs*), Siobhan Fallon (*Beatrice*), Mike Nussbaum (*Gentle Rosenberg*), Jon Gries (*Van driver*), Sergio Calderon (*Jose*), Carel Struycken (*Arquillian*), Fredrick Lane (*INS Agent Janus*), Richard Hamilton (*D*), Kent Faulcon (*First Lt. Jake Jensen*), John Alexander (*Mikey*), Keith Cambell (*Perp*), Ken Thorley (*Orkin man*), Patric Breen (*Mr. Redgick*), Becky Ann Baker (*Mrs. Redgick*), Sean Whalen (*Passport officer*), Norma Jean Groh (*Mrs. Edelson*), and Harsh Nayyar, Michael Willis, Willie C. Carpenter, Peter Linari, David Cross, Charles C. Stevenson Jr., Boris Leskin, Steve Rankin, Andy Prosky, Michael Goldfinger, Alpheus Merchant, Bernard Gilkey, Sean Plummer, Michael Kaliski, Richard Arthur, Debbie Lee Carrington, Verne Troyer, Mykal Wayne Williams.

CREDITS

A MacDonald/Parkes production. *Executive producer*, Steven Spielberg; *producers*, Walter F. Parkes and Laurie MacDonald; *coproducer*, Graham Place; *director*, Barry Sonnenfeld; *screenplay and screen story*, Ed Solomon; *based on the* Malibu Comic *by* Lowell Cunningham; *cinematographer*, Don Peterman; *production designer*, Bo Welch; *costume designer*, Mary E. Vogt; *alien makeup effects*, Rick Baker; *visual effects supervisor*, Eric Brevig; *music*, Danny Elfman; *editor*, Jim Miller. Panavision and Technicolor; *running time*, 98 minutes.

MEN IN BLACK: Alias Smith and Jones, keeping out the scum of the universe and monitoring all things alien on Earth. (photo: Melinda Sue Gordon)

In black suit and Ray-Ban shades, reverting to his no-non-sense kick-butt mode, and toting an awfully big firearm, ultracool Tommy Lee Jones turns up with similarly attired sidekick Will Smith looking like the Blues Brothers (with oversized guns in place of killer guitars). Ever vigilant and on the lookout for illegal aliens—the intergalactic kind—they keep the good, hard-working extraterrestrials inhabiting the Big Apple in line. Made primarily in New York City in early 1996 prior to Jones's West Coast *Volcano*, this unexpectedly cheerful and wonderfully engaging "*Ghostbusters* of another kind" was a live-action comic book dealing with the MiB, an elite, highly-funded, but unofficial government agency. MiB's appar-ently alphabetically named agents—mainly, in this case, Smith and Jones (as J and K)—are dedicated to, as the film's promotion ad line trumpets, "protecting the earth from the scum of the universe!" Rip Torn is around to out-bark Jones as the dyspeptic head of the MiB home office; Linda Fiorentino puts smoldering sex into running the city morgue and doing some enticing, along with the slic-ing and dicing.

Both outlandish and hip, *Men in Black* spotlights a whole 'nother side of Tommy Lee—one with a sense of humor masked in a completely deadpan character that makes Jack Webb's Sgt. Joe Friday come across as a stand-up comedian. ("Anyone doubting Jones's comic talents," David Hunter pointed out in his *Hollywood Reporter* review, "will find many hilarious examples to the contrary.") Working with both loosey-goosey ex-rap-per Smith and a gaggle of alien critters that look like refugees from *The Muppet Show* by way of *Beetle Juice*, Jones puts his craggy reserve into overdrive while never creasing the standard MiB issue black suit or smudging the spit-polished black shoes—except following a cli-mactic encounter with a truly ugly outer space creature who has gobbled him up and then is forced to spit him out, leaving him covered with goo as if he was a survivor of a Three Stooges pie fight. (This spectacularly staged sequence was shot at the site of the 1964 World's Fair in Flushing, Queens, making terrific use of the remaining pieces of architecture, just as an earlier episode, involv-ing Will Smith, took dizzying advantage of the Guggenheim Museum.)

MiB's genesis was an apparently little-known comic book series, with an underground cult following, created by Lowell Cunningham, a free-lance writer from Knoxville, Tennessee. *The Men in Black* dates back to the early 1990s, and is loosely based on urban UFO legends, which Cunningham supposedly absorbed as a kid through a 1953 issue of the journal of the International Flying Saucer Bureau, *Space Review*.

The basic plot of the film—between quips, alien encounters at the MiB coffee machine, masterful many-armed manipulations of headquarters' main computer by twin extraterrestrial octopus-like creatures named Harmon and Killebrew, and awesome explosions and set pieces—has Mr. Smith and Mr. Jones (as anony-mously identified in the advertisements) seeking to track down an intergalactic bad guy lumbering around Manhattan in search of a jewel—a marble-sized galaxy—in the possession of an exiled prince from the planet Arquillia, which is somewhere in another galaxy far, far away—but that's another movie. Their search of offbeat neighborhoods in the Big Apple has Mr. Smith (an MiB recruit from the N.Y.P.D.) cautiously inquiring of Mr. Jones why the aliens have chosen his town in which to settle down as productive members of society, and why the city has become sort of a holding pen for intergalac-tic refugees. The unflappable Tommy Lee points out, "Remember *Casablanca*? Same thing, except for the Nazis." And later, an incredulous Will Smith watches as Tommy Lee hilariously shakes down (quite literally) a talking pooch, who has a definite lead as to their quarry. He also shows his partner and protégé the technique of

MEN IN BLACK: The Men in Black visit Linda Fiorentino's morgue to examine the body of an alien in disguise. (photo: Melinda Sue Gordon)

eliminating the memory of a citizen who stumbled across too much information by whipping out a "neuralizer," a cigar-shaped pocket-pen type instrument with beeping lights, and, after coolly donning his Ray-Bans, zapping the inquisitive alien encounterer with a blinding laser beam.

Exceptionally kind reviews and a hugely marketable product (with all manner of MiB tchotchkes and a prospective animated TV cartoon series to follow, as well as probable sequels—most likely without Tommy Lee) easily made *Men in Black* the big movie hit of summer 1997, outdistancing even *Batman and Robin* at the box office. In its first week of release, it made back a huge chunk of its not-exactly-peanuts budget. Critic Susan Wioszczyna, in her four-star *USA Today* review, labeled the film a "snappy, sci-fi hoot . . . a kind of *Independence Day* for smart people" and (apparently lovingly) found Jones to be "crusty as burnt toast . . . [He] likes to refer to aliens as 'our friends from out of town.'" Janet Maslin, in the *New York Times*, found *Men in Black* to be "dryly clever" and admired Tommy Lee Jones for being "supremely unruffled, tacitly hilarious."

MEN IN BLACK: Cool Ray-Banned agents K (Jones) and J (Smith) "neuralize" a witness to an alien encounter. (photo: Melinda Sue Gordon)

TELEVISION

While in New York, beginning in 1970 and following his days at Harvard, Tom Lee Jones did some live television, making his debut on *Directions* on ABC, a weekly Sunday morning religious program. "Sunday Dinner," a twenty-five-minute episode, broadcast on February 1, 1970, had him playing a young married man in conflict with his bride (played by Lana Shaw) over which religion to embrace.

From 1971 to 1975 he was seen as Dr. Mark Toland on the ABC soap opera *One Life to Live* before going to the West Coast. As Tommy Lee Jones, his first TV work in Hollywood was in the episode "Fatal Witness," on *Barnaby Jones* on CBS (November 14, 1975), as a doctor accused of murder, and in the "Dead Man Out" episode of *Baretta* on ABC (March 3, 1976), as the guest heavy of the week, among other series work. He had a pivotal role in the ninety-minute *Charlie's Angels* TV-movie pilot on ABC (March 21, 1976), playing one Aram Kolegian, and then he was a motorcycle cop in the all-star car-crash TV movie *Smash-up on Interstate 5* on ABC (December 3, 1976). Both were directed by John Llewellyn Moxey.

Following are Tommy Lee Jones's starring roles on television.

30

THE AMAZING HOWARD HUGHES

CBS, APRIL 13–14, 1977

CAST

Tommy Lee Jones (*Howard Hughes*), Ed Flanders (*Noah Dietrich*), James Hampton (*Wilbur Peterson*), Tovah Feldshuh (*Katharine Hepburn*), Lee Purcell (*Billie Dove*), Jim Antonio (*George*), Sorrell Booke (*Fiorello La Guardia*), Marty Brill (*Lewis Milestone*), Marla Carlis (*Jane Russell*), Lee Jones-DeBroux (*Jimmy*), Roy Engel (*Production Manager*), Arthur Franz (*Barnes*), Denise Galik (*Shirley Whitehead*), Howard Hesseman (*Jenks*), Tannis G. Montgomery (*Mrs. Hughes*), Walter O. Miles (*Gen. Hap Arnold*), Garry Walberg (*Henry J. Kaiser*), Carol Bagdasarian (*Jean Peters*), Bart Burns (*Robert Maheu*), Thayer David (*Floyd Odlum*), Morgan Brittany (*Ella Hughes*), Susan Buckner (*Jean Harlow*), Ray Buktenica (*PR Man*), Ed Harris (*Russ*), and Barry Atwater, William Dozier, James Bacon, John S. Ragin, John Lupton, Art Gilmore, Ray Ballard, Robert Baron, James Beach, Sid Conrad, Jack Denbo, Wayne Heffley, Dave Shelley, Wayne Thomis, Jerome Thor, Myron Natwick, Andy Romano.

CREDITS

A Roger Gimbel production for EMI Television. *Executive producer:* Roger Gimbel; *producers,* Herbert Hirschman and Paul Cameron; *director,* William A. Graham; *teleplay,* John Gay; *based on the book* Howard, the Amazing Mr. Hughes, *by* Noah Dietrich and Bob Thomas; *photography,* Michael Margulies and Jules Brenner; *music,* Laurence Rosenthal; *editors,* Aaron Stell and Michael S. McLean.

As the enigmatic Howard Hughes, from an eighteen-year-old stripling when he took control of Hughes Tool Company to reclusive old billionaire, Tommy Lee Jones made the most of a plum role that forced reviewers and television viewers to take notice. It is the part that, in effect, "made" Tommy Lee. His resemblance to fellow Texan Hughes, with thin mustache, twenty less pounds, and minimal makeup except for Hughes's declining years, was truly uncanny—helping greatly to foster the illusion. So did the parade of familiar film figures, from Jean Harlow and Billie Dove to Katharine Hepburn (played well by relatively diminutive Tovah Feldshuh, who overcame the height disparity with the real Kate), Jane Russell, and Jean Peters, the fifties actress who dropped out of films to become Mrs. Hughes.

"People often ask me if it is easier to play a real-life character than a fictional one," Jones later said. "The conventional answer is that it is much better to play a real character because the physical characteristics have established patterns—a walk, speech patterns, and such. When you play someone like Hughes, there is a wealth of information about almost every day in his life. For a recluse, he was probably the most documented hermit in the world."

Others who subsequently played Howard Hughes on film are Jason Robards as the aged Hughes in Jonathan Demme's *Melvin and Howard* (1980) and Dean Stockwell (to whom Tommy Lee Jones bears some resemblance) as middle-aged Hughes in Francis Ford Coppola's *Tucker: The Man and His Dream* (1988).

THE AMAZING HOWARD HUGHES (1977): As Hughes, the eccentric moviemaker of the thirties . . .

. . . and the reclusive billionaire of the seventies

BARN BURNING (1980): **Tommy Lee Jones** as Abner Snopes, Faulkner's aggrieved arsonist

31

BARN BURNING

AMERICAN SHORT STORY

PBS, MARCH 18, 1980

CAST

Tommy Lee Jones (*Abner Snopes*), Diane Kagan (*Mother Snopes*), Carolyn Coates (*Lula De Spain*), Michael Riney (*Brother*), Shawn Whittington (*Sarty Snopes*), Jimmy Faulkner (*Major De Spain*), and Jennie Hughes, Julie Kaye Townery, Al Scott, Jean Pettigrew.

CREDITS

A Learning in Focus production. *Executive producer,* Robert Geller; *producer,* Calvin Skaggs; *director,* Peter Werner; *teleplay,* Horton Foote; *photography,* Peter Sova; *music,* Elizabeth Swados; *art director,* Patrizia von Brandenstein; *editor,* Jay Freund.

In this forty-five-minute adaptation of William Faulkner's 1939 tale, part of a double bill on PBS's *American Short Story* series, Jones is the surly itinerant tenant farmer with a habit of burning down the barns of unfriendly landlords, sparking a crisis of conscience in his young son, who wants to end the arson. Unlike an earlier television version in the mid-fifties, adapted by Gore Vidal and directed by Robert Mulligan for the *Suspense* series and starring E. G. Marshall and Beatrice Straight, this later production was set in the late 1800s.

THE RAINMAKER (1982): Blown into a drought-ridden area in the Midwest with a promise to make it rain for $100

32

THE RAINMAKER

HBO, OCTOBER 24, 1982

CAST

Tommy Lee Jones (*Starbuck*), Tuesday Weld (*Lizzie Curry*), William Katt (*Jimmy Curry*), James Cromwell (*Noah Curry*), Lonny Chapman (*H. C. Curry*), Taylor Larcher (*File*), William Traylor (*Sheriff Thomas*).

CREDITS

A Paramount Pictures Television production. *Producer*, Marcia Govons; *director*, John Frankenheimer; *based on the play by* N. Richard Nash; *sets*, Rosaia Sinisi.

This not-widely-seen adaptation for cable TV of the play about a Depression-era con man who traveled the back roads of parched middle America with promises of bringing much-needed rain and the impact he made on a local spinster and the family that was trying for years to marry her off provided another expansive showcase for Tommy Lee.

Although best remembered as a movie that teamed Burt Lancaster and Katharine Hepburn, *The Rainmaker* originated as a television play on NBC's *Philco Playhouse* in August 1953 with Darren McGavin and Joan Potter. It then was produced on Broadway the following year, with McGavin repeating his role as Starbuck, opposite Geraldine Page. The original TV version, the play, and the movie were all directed by Joseph Anthony. There was also a West End stage version in 1956, with Geraldine Page again playing the spinster role and Sam Wanamaker as Starbuck. In 1963 a musical version called *110 in the Shade* (by composers Harvey Schmidt and Tom Jones) opened on Broadway and ran for about a year. Inga Swenson and Robert Horton starred, and Joseph Anthony once again directed.

The 1977 taped production, which teamed Tommy Lee Jones and Tuesday Weld and returned onetime directing wunderkind John Frankenheimer to television after a number of fallow big-screen years, has never been made available for home video. For the record, Burt Reynolds directed a version in 1979 of *The Rainmaker* at his dinner theater in Jupiter, Florida, and played Starbuck opposite Sally Field.

Starbuck forecasting optimistic weather for lonely Lizzie Curry (Tuesday Weld)

33

THE EXECUTIONER'S SONG

NBC, NOVEMBER 28–29, 1982

CAST

Tommy Lee Jones (*Gary Gilmore*), Rosanna Arquette (*Nicole Baker*), Christine Lahti (*Brenda Nicol*), Eli Wallach (*Uncle Vern Damico*), Jordan Clarke (*Johnny Nicol*), Steve Keats (*Larry Samuels*), Richard Venture (*Earl Dorius*), Jenny Wright (*April Baker*), Walter Olkewicz (*Pete Galovan*), Michael LeClair (*Rikki Wood*), Grace Zabriskie (*Kathryne Baker*), Pat Corley (*Val Conlan*), Mary Gregory (*Ida Damico*), John Dennis Johnston (*Jimmy Poker-Game*), Norris Church (*LuAnn*), Kenneth O'Brien (*Spencer McGrath*), Jim Youngs (*Sterling Baker*), Rance Howard (*Lieutenant Nielsen*), Charles Cyphers (*Noall Wootton*), and John Chappell, Ray Girardin, Grant Gottschall, Mark Campbell, Kathryn Whitehead, Bruce Newbold, Babetta Dick, Sharon Lehner, Angie Sorenson, Victoria Jean, H. E. D. Redford.

CREDITS

A Lawrence Schiller production for NBC Television; *producer-director*, Lawrence Schiller; *supervising producer*, John Thomas Lenox; *teleplay*, Norman Mailer, *based on his book*; *photography*, Freddie Francis; *production designer*, Jac McAnelly; *music*, John Cacavas; *songs*, Waylon Jennings; *editors*, Richard A. Harris and Tom Rolfe.

The role of Gary Gilmore, lowlife mid-1970s Utah killer who fought efforts to prevent his execution and demanded to be put to death by a firing squad, brought Tommy Lee Jones his first Emmy Award as Outstanding Actor. His riveting performance in this two-part, four-hour version of Norman Mailer's Pulitzer Prize–winning book, covering the period between April 1976 and January 1977, which included the time of Gilmore's parole (he'd served twelve years in Illinois for armed robbery) and the multiple robbery–murders then committed until the time of his death, demonstrated Jones's acting range, and it still stands as one of his career highlights. The depiction of Gilmore's relationship with Nicole Baker, a trampish teenage divorcée (played with earthy glee by Rosanna Arquette, who also received an Emmy nomination), broke new ground for network television. In the theatrical version shown in Europe (cut by more than an hour) and currently available on home video, many of their scenes contained a great deal of nudity.

As dead-ender Gary Gilmore

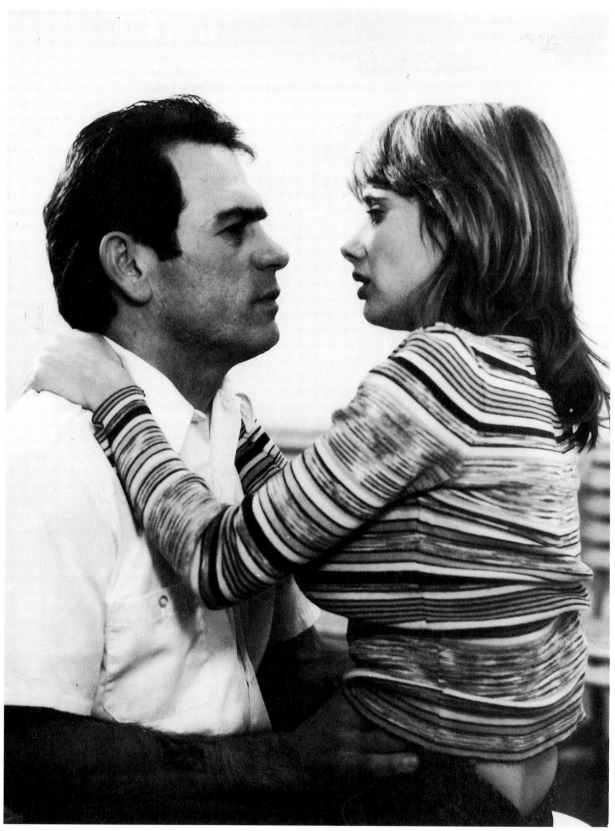

Tommy Lee Jones as loser Gary Gilmore and Rosanna Arquette as earthy Nicole Baker

Eyes of a killer who demands to die

34

CAT ON A HOT TIN ROOF

SHOWTIME (*BROADWAY ON SHOWTIME*),
AUGUST 19, 1984;
PBS (*AMERICAN PLAYHOUSE*),
JUNE 24, 1985

CAST

Jessica Lange (*Maggie*), Tommy Lee Jones (*Brick*), Rip Torn (*Big Daddy*), Kim Stanley (*Big Mama*), David Dukes (*Gooper*), Penny Fuller (*Mae*), Macon McCalman (*Reverend Tooker*), Fran Bennett (*Sookey*), Jack Jundeff (*Buster*), Thomas Hill (*Dr. Braugh*), Netta-Lee Noy (*Sonny*).

CREDITS

A production of International Television Group (ITG) and KCET, Los Angeles. *Executive producer,* Lou LaMonte; *producer,* Phyllis Heller; *director,* Jack Hofsiss; *adapted from the play by* Tennessee Williams; *production designer,* John Retsek; *music,* Tom Scott

In his portrayal of Brick in *Cat on a Hot Tin Roof,* Tommy Lee Jones imbued the character with more homosexuality than was offered by Ben Gazzara and his successors in the various stage versions beginning in 1955, by Paul Newman in the whitewashed 1958 movie, and by Robert Wagner in Laurence Olivier's 1976 television adaptation. This production incorporated the alternate ending that

Tennessee Williams provided for the 1974 Broadway revival that teamed Elizabeth Ashley and Keir Dullea.

Brooding, drinking, hobbling around on a crutch, ignoring sexually aggressive wife Maggie's (Jessica Lange, who would later again act opposite Tommy Lee in *Blue Sky*) prowling advances, Jones remains sullen through much of the first act, exploding his inner feelings at last to Big Daddy (Rip Torn) about his obsession with his dead friend Skipper, which means more to him than his marriage to Maggie. This version had an unusual history: In a unique arrangement, it premiered initially on cable TV and later was broadcast on regular television on PBS, which was involved in the initial production. Big Mama here was played by Kim Stanley, coming out of semiretirement. She had initially played Maggie the Cat in the 1958 London production.

CAT ON A HOT TIN ROOF (1984): Brick and Maggie (Jessica Lange) discuss their troubled marriage.

Big Daddy (Rip Torn) faces down pathetic son Brick, who confesses his demons.

35

THE PARK IS MINE

HBO, OCTOBER 6, 1985

CAST

Tommy Lee Jones (*Mitch Harris*), Helen Shaver (*Valery Weaver*), Yaphet Kotto (*Capt. Frank Eubanks*), Eric Peterson (*Mike Kuhn*), Lawrence Dane (*Commander Keller*), Peter Dvorsky (*Deputy Mayor Dix*), Dennis Simpson (*Richie*), Reg Dreger (*Commander Curran*), Louis DiBianco (*Captain Juliano*), Gale Garnett (*Rachel*).

CREDITS

An Astral Film Enterprises production for HBO Premiere Films. *Executive producers,* Harold Greenberg and Claude Heroux; *producer,* Denis Heroux; *director,* Steven Hilliard Stern; *teleplay,* Lyle Gorch; *based on the novel by* Stephen Peters; *photography,* Laszlo George; *art director,* François DeLucy; *music,* Tangerine Dream; *editor,* Ron Sanders.

Playing an unstable, jobless Vietnam vet whose homeless buddy has committed suicide out of despair, Tommy Lee decides to take over New York's Central Park for seventy-two hours over the Veteran's Day weekend in a symbolic protest to spotlight the plight of veterans. Donning his army fatigues and painting himself with jungle camouflage, he mines the park. (The entire film was shot in Toronto.) He quickly gets the attention of initially skeptical city authorities and the media, represented by Yaphet Kotto as a police captain and Helen

THE PARK IS MINE (1985): Jones as an unemployed, divorced Vietnam vet who dons war gear and seals off Central Park to make a statement

Shaver as an intrepid TV reporter who manages to sneak into the park, maneuver around the booby traps, and get to the "kidnapper" for an up-close interview. He tells her he doesn't intend to hurt anybody—he just wants people to listen—and then indulges in polemics. "Jones is strong," TV critic Kay Gardella (New York *Daily News*) wrote, "but he should have had enough training to avoid the worst booby trap of all: the script."

Newscaster Helen Shaver makes her way into Central Park to meet with emotionally shattered veteran Tommy Lee Jones.

36

YURI NOSENKO, KGB

HBO, SEPTEMBER 7, 1986

CAST

Tommy Lee Jones (*Steve Daley*), Oleg Rudnik (*Yuri Nosenko*), Josef Sommer (*James Angelton*), Ed Lauter (*Jerry Tyler*), George Morforgen (*Anatoli Golitsyn*), Stephen D. Newman (*Ed Douglas*), Alexandra O'Karma (*Anna Daley*), Christopher Wynkoop (*Richard Helms*), Edwin Adams (*John Collins*), Michael DeSanto (*Kenny Klein*), Kevin Cooney (*Don Fisher*), Irwin Ziff (*Soviet speaker*), H. Richard Greene (*John Rogers*), Austin Leonard Jones (*Tom Daley*), James Hornbeck (*James McDonald*), Pat Richardson (*Joan Black*), Eugene Troobnick (*Frank Lewis*), and Dani Dalain, Phil Gaines, David Healy, Pamela Roussel, Blaise Corrigan, Dan Dimmick, John Ortman.

CREDITS

A production of BBC Television and Primetime Television Ltd. *Executive producer*, David Elstein; *producer*, Graham Massey; *director*, Mick Jackson; *teleplay*, Stephen Davis; *photography*, David Feig; *production designer*, Paul Joel; *music*, Peter Howell; *editor*, Jim Latham.

Yuri Nosenko, a real-life Russian agent who came in from the cold not long after the assassination of John F. Kennedy and tried to get the United States to believe he

YURI NOSENKO, KGB (1986): Spies on opposite sides find themselves together in Washington: Oleg Rudnik as a KGB defector and Tommy Lee Jones as a dubious CIA agent.

was honestly looking to defect, becomes the concern of U.S. Intelligence, which has concluded he is looking to plant information and confuse the government. CIA agent Steve Daley (a fictitious name) is called on to decide whether Nosenko is for real or a red herring, and thus a cat-and-mouse game plays itself out between Oleg Rudnik, a Russian actor who emigrated to America in the seventies, and Jones. "Tommy Lee Jones provides a masterful portrait of Steve Daley . . . who suspects that Nosenko is a KGB plant," reviewer Laurel Gross wrote in the *New York Post*. And Miles Beller said in *The Hollywood Reporter:* "Jones gives one of the strongest acting jobs of his career, understated and smartly realized." *People* magazine's Jeff Jarvis found that "Jones usually acts without changing his expression, but that makes him the perfect spy."

Tommy Lee's son, Austin, had a small role as his on-screen son in this British-made cold war spy thriller.

37

BROKEN VOWS

CBS, JANUARY 28, 1987

CAST

Tommy Lee Jones (*Joseph McMahon*), Annette O'Toole (*Nim Fitzpatrick*), M. Emmet Walsh (*Detective Mulligan*), Milo O'Shea (*Monsignor Casey*), David Groh (*Mason Drumm*), Madeleine Sherwood (*Mrs. Chase*), Jean De Baer (*Gena Drumm*), David Strathairn (*Stuart Chase*), Frances Fisher (*Maureen Phelan*), Peter Crombie (*Dan Phelan*), and Anthony LaGuerre, Sylvia Short, Richard Dumont, Andrew Nichols, Joseph Drblik, Mark Kulik.

CREDITS

Robert Halmi, Inc. in association with Brademan-Shelf Productions. *Executive producers*, Peter Zinner and Robert C. Thompson; *producers*, Bill Brademan and Ed Self; *supervising producer*, Robert Halmi; *director*, Jud Taylor; *teleplay*, Ivan Davis [pseudonym for James Costigan]; *based on the novel* Where the Dark Streets Go *by* Dorothy Salisbury Davis; *photography*, Thomas Burstyn; *production designer*, Jocelyn Joy; *music*, Charles Gross; *editor*, Norman Gay.

Tommy Lee Jones, with his increasingly strong presence, is a parish priest whose faith is tested when he finds himself involved in a murder after being summoned to give last rites to a stabbing victim, a stranger who lies dying in an abandoned tenement. With the dead man's girl-friend (played by Annette O'Toole), he begins a search

BROKEN VOWS (1987): As a parish priest in a crisis of conscience

for the killer, but throughout the investigation a developing relationship with the woman causes him to question his vows of celibacy and eventually his position in the priesthood.

The story, which bears some plot resemblance to Alfred Hitchcock's *I Confess*, was adapted from Dorothy Salisbury Davis's novel *Where the Dark Streets Go* by veteran screenwriter James Costigan, who at the last minute had his name removed from the credits. *Variety*'s critic said: "*Broken Vows* fails to make a Roman Catholic priest's weaknesses and decisions much more than dramatic devices. . . . The deliberate manner in which Jones and O'Toole visually bed down is only one of the unnecessary offenses [and] the telefilm's murder mystery becomes secondary, an appendage, while O'Toole and Jones make no visible efforts to resist physical urges."

Tommy Lee Jones becomes involved with Annette O'Toole while investigating the murder of her boyfriend.

38

STRANGER ON MY LAND

ABC, JANUARY 17, 1988

CAST

Tommy Lee Jones (*Buddy Whitman*), Dee Wallace Stone (*Annie Whitman*), Ben Johnson (*Vern Whitman*), Terry O'Quinn (*Connie Priest*), Pat Hingle (*Judge Munson*), Barry Corbin (*Gil Rosine*), Richard Anderson (*Major Walters*), Ned Romero (*Doc*), Natalie Gregory (*Gillie Whitman*), Lyman Ward (*Doug Whitman*), Paul Chan (*Eliot Song*), Kent Williams (*Judge*), Joseph Gordon Levitt (*Rounder*), Annie O'Connell (*Mrs. Fourchette*), Michael Flynn (*Brewer*), Tip Boxell (*Captain Wister*), Eric Hart (*Gil Worthy*), and John Daryl, Michael Ruud, George Sullivan, Jeff Allin, Arsenio "Sonny" Trinidad, Tien Long, John Perryman, Alan Nash, Jeff Olson, Mike Watkiss, Tim Nelson, Marshall Bill Turner, Bill Shanks.

CREDITS

Edgar J. Scherick Associates and Taft Entertainment Television. *Executive producers,* Edgar J. Scherick and Gary Hoffman; *producer,* Michael Barnathan; *director,* Larry Elikann; *teleplay,* Edward Hume and I. C. Rappaport, *from a story by* Hume; *photography,* Laszlo George; *production designer,* Michael Baugh; *music,* Ron Ramin; *editor,* Peter V. White.

STRANGER ON MY LAND (1988): Tommy Lee Jones and Dee Wallace Stone as Vietnam vet and wife, standing tall against Uncle Sam

In this old-fashioned Western masquerading in contemporary garb, Jones plays a Vietnam veteran who has returned to his life as a rancher—his spread has been in his family for generations—and slowly turns into a Rambo when the government exercises its right to take over the land for a missile base. He and his father (played by Ben Johnson) refuse all offers to sell the land, rebuff all court orders to vacate, and drive off anyone crossing the property line. "Progress is going to stop at my gate," Jones tells Uncle Sam. Gunplay eventually ensues, and Tommy Lee is at war again in a Ruby Ridge–like standoff. *Variety's* critic felt that "with Tommy Lee Jones lending his strong presence to the proceedings, vidpic has lots to say, says it, and sits down."

Initially called *Eminent Domain*, this 1988 telefilm was reminiscent of the earlier *Fire on the Mountain* (1981), in which Ron Howard and Buddy Ebsen fight Uncle Sam over whether the family land is to be replaced by an army missile base.

Onetime Oscar winner Ben Johnson and future Oscar winner Tommy Lee Jones as father and son, taking a stand on their land

Tommy Lee Jones and Chad Lowe as father and son

39

APRIL MORNING

HALLMARK HALL OF FAME

CBS, APRIL 24, 1988

CAST

Tommy Lee Jones (*Moses Cooper*), Robert Urich (*Joseph Simmons*), Chad Lowe (*Adam Cooper*), Susan Blakely (*Susan Cooper*), Rip Torn (*Solomon Chandler*), Joan Heney (*Granny Cooper*), Nicholas Kilbertus (*John Parker*), Griffith Brewer (*Samuel Hadley*), Thor Bishopric (*Jonathan Harrington*), Joel Miller (*Reverend*), Brian Furlong (*Joash Smith*), Anthony Ulc (*Simon Caspar*), Philip Spensley (*John Buckman*), Peter Colvey (*Maj. John Pitcairn*), Gary Plaxton (*Lt. Col. Francis Smith*), Vlasta Vrana (*Paul Revere*), and Jeannie Walker, Alan Mozes, John Baggaley, Burke Lawrence, Paul Rutledge, Ken Siegel, David Gow, Teddy Lee Dillon, James Coull, Timothy Hine, Vincent Glorioso.

CREDITS

Robert Halmi, Inc. in association with the Samuel Goldwyn Company. *Executive producers*, Robert Halmi and Samuel Goldwyn Jr.; *supervising producer*, David J. Patterson; *producers*, Robert Halmi Jr. and Delbert Mann; *director*, Delbert Mann; *teleplay*, James Lee Barrett; *based on the novel by* Howard Fast; *photography*, Frank Tidy; *production designer*, William Beeton; *music*, Allyn Ferguson; *editor*, Eric Albertson.

Howard Fast's 1961 novel about the day the first shot of the American Revolution was fired on Lexington Green and the effect on a New England family and fellow colonials came to television with a batch of anachronisms with which veteran director Delbert Mann (one of the greats from TV's Golden Age of live drama) and the talented cast, headed by Tommy Lee Jones, had to contend. Tommy Lee was an American colonist of British descent—as he explains to Chad Lowe, as his brooding teenage son, during a heart-to-heart—whose Texas drawl was a bit disconcerting (since Texas did not exist at the time other than as a Spanish province somewhere south of the uncharted North American continent). The production was filmed entirely on the outskirts of Toronto, which apparently had maintained the outdoor, stonewalled look of rural eighteenth-century Massachusetts.

April Morning was lyrically crafted by screenwriter James Lee Barrett into a *Hallmark Hall of Fame* coming-of-age tale of a youngster who had spent his entire young life trying to please his strict, relentless, somewhat distant dad and finally, on that fateful morning of April 19, 1775, has the opportunity to stand shoulder to shoulder with him as they and other minutemen make their stand against the British redcoats following Paul Revere's alert. Tommy Lee Jones would be the first casualty of the war. Critic John Leonard wrote in *New York* magazine: "While [he] is still around, his diction takes some getting used to, a kind of biblical/Eastwood prophetic utterance, but it seems to work when he's telling God how to go about His business."

APRIL MORNING (1988): "Minuteman" Tommy Lee Jones with family and fellow colonists on the eve of the American Revolution: (*from left*) Susan Blakely, Chad Lowe, Meredith Salenger, Robert Urich, and the rabble-rousing Rip Torn

Grieving wife, Susan Blakely, mourns the first victim of American Revolution.

199

40

GOTHAM

SHOWTIME, AUGUST 21, 1988

CAST

Tommy Lee Jones (*Eddie Martel Mallard*), Virginia Madsen (*Rachel Carlyle*), Colin Bruce (*Charlie Rand*), Denise Stephenson (*Debbie*), Kevin Jarre (*Tim*), Frederic Forrest (*Father George*), J. B. White (*Jimbo*), Michael Chapman (*Landlord*), Alec Willows (*Bartender*), Jack Creley (*Grandfather*), Peter Jobin (*Doorman*), Michael Villela (*Cop*), David Cryer (*Waiter*), Holly Johnson (*Singer*), Hugh McCarten (*Piano player*).

CREDITS

A Keith Addis & Associates production in association with Phoenix Entertainment Group. *Executive producers,* Gerald I. Eisenberg and Keith Addis; *producers,* David Latt and Eli Johnson; *writer-director,* Lloyd Fonvielle; *photography,* Michael Chapman; *production designer,* Carol Spier; *music,* George S. Clinton; *editor,* Evan Lottman.

GOTHAM (1988): The nickel-and-dime Gotham gumshoe

Tommy Lee Jones stars as down-on-his-luck shamus Edward "Call me Eddie" Mallard in this odd noirish amalgam of gumshoe and the supernatural. Eddie is hired by a mousy guy named Charlie Rand to find his sultry wife, who was killed ten years earlier in a boating accident but has now come back to haunt him for the jewelry she claims he owes her. Hard-boiled Eddie takes the odd case because the money's good and soon finds himself suckered by the spectacular-looking, high-heeled femme fatale Rachel Carlyle and drifts into a steamy affair with this red-blooded ghost, who likes to shed her clothes. (She was supposed to be buried naked with the gems, she tells him.) All this—like finding Rachel slumbering comfortably inside his refrigerator and himself becoming enmeshed in a philosophical discussion with a Russian Orthodox priest who wanders in and out—made for one enigmatic misfire.

Hot-blooded ghost Virginia Madsen puts the make on down-on-his-luck dick Tommy Lee Jones.

The Gotham shamus

41

LONESOME DOVE

CBS, FEBRUARY 5–8, 1989

CAST

Robert Duvall (*Capt. Gus McCrae*), Tommy Lee Jones (*Capt. Woodrow F. Call*), Danny Glover (*Joshua Deets*), Diane Lane (*Lorena Wood*), Robert Urich (*Jake Spoon*), Frederic Forrest (*Blue Duck*), D. B. Sweeney (*Dish Boggett*), Rick Schroder (*Newt Dobbs*), Anjelica Huston (*Clara Allen*), Chris Cooper (*Sheriff July Johnson*), Tim Scott (*Pea-Eye Parker*), Glenne Headley (*Elmira Johnson*), Barry Corbin (*Deputy Roscoe Brown*), William Sanderson (*Lippy Jones*), Barry Tubb (*Jasper Fant*), Gavin O'Herlihy (*Dan Suggs*), Steve Buscemi (*Luke*), Frederic Coffin (*Big Zwey*), Travis Swords (*Allen O'Brien*), Kevin O'Morrison (*Doctor*), Ron Weyand (*Old Hugh*), Leon Singer (*Bolivar*), Lanny Flaherty (*Soupy Jones*), Pierre Epstein (*Xavier Wanz*), David Carpenter (*Needle Johnson*), Helena Humann (*Peach Johnson*), Adam Faraizl (*Joe Boot*), Nina Siemasko (*Janey*), O-Lan Jones (*Sally Skull*), Nada Despotovich (*Mary*), and John Quijada, Max Evers, Wallace Merck, Jimmy Pickens, Robert Donley, David Ode, Paul James Vasques, Brandon Smith, Jordan Lund, Matthew Posey, Michael Tylo, Margo Martindale, Jorge Martinez de Hoyos, Jerry Biggs, Sean Hennigan, Julius Tennon, David Carpenter, Thomas Connor, Missy Crider, James McMurtry, Charlie Haynie, Sonny Carl Davis, Terry McIlvain, Tony Epper.

CREDITS

Motown Productions in association with Pangaea and Qintex Entertainment Inc. *Executive producers*, Suzanne de Passe and Bill Wittliff; *coexecutive producer*, Robert Halmi

LONESOME DOVE (1989): As ex-Texas Ranger Woodrow Call

Jr.; *supervising producer*, Michael Wiesbarth; *producer*, Dyson Lovell; *director*, Simon Wincer; *teleplay*, Bill Wittliff; *based on the novel by* Larry McMurtry; *photography*, Douglas Milsome; *production designer*, Cary White; *music*, Basil Poledouris; *editor*, Corky Ehlers.

In the first of Tommy Lee Jones's two (to date) television Westerns, an eight-hour, four-part version of Larry McMurtry's epic tale, he costars as taciturn, restless, occasionally grumpy, white-haired-and-bearded Woodrow Call, an ex–Texas Ranger turned rancher with his philosophical, more voluble Ranger pal Gus McCrae. The two, who operate the Hat Creek Outfit in the Texas town of Lonesome Dove, a small cattle and livery outfit staffed by a motley crew, strike out on an adventurous cattle drive to uncharted Montana Territory.

The success of the miniseries, which garnered eighteen Emmy nominations (including Best Actor for both

Woodrow Call pays a visit to partner Gus McCrae's old flame, Clara Allen (Anjelica Huston).

Tommy Lee Jones and Robert Duvall), encouraged CBS to commission an "unauthorized" sequel, titled *Return to Lonesome Dove*—with which McMurtry had nothing to do. The Jones role of Call was played by Jon Voight. (Duvall's McCrae died in the original.) This was followed by the syndicated *Lonesome Dove—The Series*, later titled *Lonesome Dove—The Outlaw Years*, which did not employ the Jones character. In late 1995, McMurtry's "true" sequel, *Streets of Laredo*, premiered, with James Garner now playing the role of Woodrow Call.

Tommy Lee won a second Emmy nomination for this epic Western.

42

THE GOOD OLD BOYS

TNT, MARCH 5, 1995

CAST

Tommy Lee Jones (*Hewey Calloway*), Sissy Spacek (*Spring Renfro*), Sam Shepard (*Snort Yarnell*), Frances McDormand (*Eve Calloway*), Terry Kinney (*Walter Calloway*), Wilford Brimley (*C. C. Tarpley*), Walter Olkewicz (*Fat Gervin*), Matt Damon (*Cotton Calloway*), Blayne Weaver (*Tommy Calloway*), Bruce McGill (*City Marshal*), Larry Mahan (*Blue Hannigan*), Richard Jones (*Alvin Loudermilk*), Karen Jones (*Cora Loudermilk*), Park Overall (*Florence*), Laura Poe (*Betsy*), Joaquin Jackson (*Wes Wheeler*), James Harrell (*Pierson Phelps*), and Jeff Gore, Norberto Navarette, Margaret Bowman, Bernerd Engel, Larry Lynch, Rodger Boyce, Joe Sears, Tennessee, Tony Epper, Jimmy Don Cox, Cliff Teinert, Patrick Scott, Ted J. Crum, Tom Hadley, Clay M. Lindley, and Bill the Dog.

CREDITS

Edgar J. Scherick and Associates and Turner Pictures in association with Firebrand Productions and the Javalina Film Company. *Executive producer,* Edgar J. Scherick; *producer,* Salli Newman; *coproducers,* Mitch Engel and J. Matt Merritt; *director,* Tommy Lee Jones; *teleplay,* Tommy Lee Jones and J. T. Allen; *based on the novel by* Elmer Kelton; *photography,* Alan Caso; *production designer,* Cary White; *music,* John McEuen; *editor,* Kimberly Ray.

Tommy Lee and Sissy: good old Oscar-winning buddies from Texas (photo: Erik Heinila)

Schoolmarm Spring Renfro (Sissy Spacek) makes Hewey think about settling down. (photo: Lance Staedler)

Jones made his directorial debut with this turn-of-the-century Western, cowrote the script from Elmer Kelton's 1978 novel, and starred as what was described as a charming rounder caught between a rock and a hard place—the twentieth century. His Hewey Calloway is a cowboy torn between the saddle-tramp life he loves in the shrinking American West and the woman, a local schoolmarm, who makes him think about finally settling down after he returns home to visit with his brother and his family. It took a keen ear for the average viewer to decipher the Jones drawl and the local West Texas patois in this leisurely paced drama which got admiring reviews from most critics, an Emmy nomination for costar Sissy Spacek, and a CableAce nomination for Tommy Lee.

THE GOOD OLD BOYS (1995): As weary
saddle tramp Hewey Calloway (photo:
Erik Heinila)

Tommy Lee Jones, director (photo: Erik Heinila)

(photo: Ralph Nelson)